The DNA of
BENTLEY

This edition first published in 2004 by Motorbooks International,
an imprint of MBI Publishing Company, Galtier Plaza, Suite 200,
380 Jackson Street, St. Paul, MN 55101-3885 USA

Motorbooks International titles are also available at discounts in bulk quantity for industrial
or sales-promotional use. For details write to Special Sales Manager at Motorbooks International
Wholesalers & Distributors, Galtier Plaza, Suite 200, 380 Jackson Street,
St. Paul, MN 55101-3885 USA.

ISBN 0-7603-1946-4

Printed in China

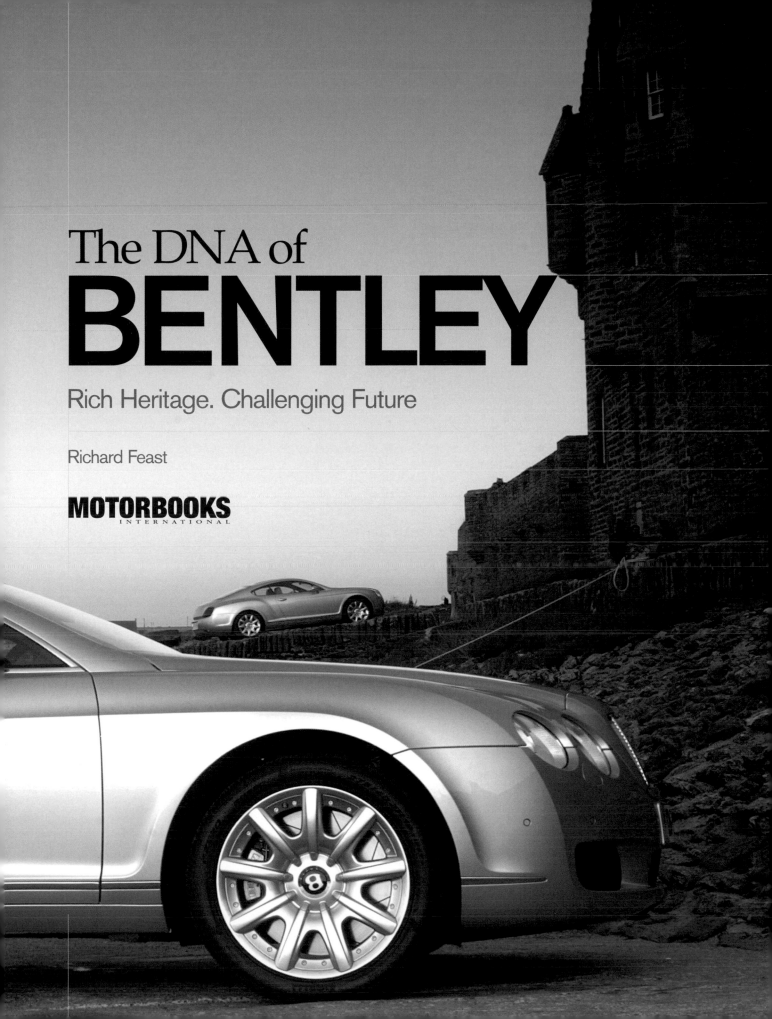

The DNA of
BENTLEY

Rich Heritage. Challenging Future

Richard Feast

MOTORBOOKS
INTERNATIONAL

Contents

Foreword   7

Chapter 1   **The legend lives again**   9

There was all-round optimism for the Continental GT when it was launched. After all, Bentley was the brand that almost died of neglect.

Chapter 2   **How the legend was born**   23

Customers liked Walter Owen Bentley's powerful 3-litres in the early 1920s. However, W.O. proved to be a better engineer than a businessman.

Chapter 3   **Vintage years**   37

Bentley Motors expanded its range with bigger and more powerful models. The legend was created, though, by motor racing successes at Le Mans.

Chapter 4   **When Barnato bought Bentley**   57

Woolf Barnato rescued Bentley, but even his great wealth was affected by the Wall Street Crash. It was the moment for Rolls-Royce to pounce.

Chapter 5   **Togetherness: Rolls-Royce/Bentley**   71

Everything changed after Bentley was bought by Rolls-Royce. W.O. was sidelined as Sir Henry Royce oversaw the design of a new Bentley range.

Chapter 6	**Rolls-Royce loses the plot**	85
	Rolls-Royce's preoccupation with aero engines only served to marginalise its car-making business. In the process, the Bentley name nearly disappeared.	
Chapter 7	**Memories are made of this**	103
	The R-type Continental coupe became one of the legendary Bentleys. True to form, Rolls-Royce failed to develop the concept with subsequent models.	
Chapter 8	**Back from the brink**	113
	The car business was separated after Rolls-Royce went bust. When the subsequent merger with Vickers led to the Bentley revival, there was no going back.	
Chapter 9	**All change**	129
	After all the turbulence, the end of the 20th century brought an even more dramatic development: Bentley and Rolls-Royce were suddenly put up for auction.	
Chapter 10	**A fresh start**	137
	The sale turned Bentley and Rolls-Royce into rivals once more. Under Volkswagen, Bentley produced a race winner, a car for a Queen and an all-new model.	
	Index	156
	Acknowledgments	160

Foreword

Immersing myself in the history of Bentley Motors for this book, it was impossible to escape the notion that the tale epitomised the broader decline of Britain's indigenous motor industry. Like so many famous marques in this country, Bentley was a cherished name with a dedicated following. Its problem was commercial failure until bought by a foreign firm.

W.O. Bentley was the gifted engineer who lacked business acumen. When his company required a bail-out – only five years after delivering its first car -- it did not simply need money. It needed someone in charge with a deep understanding of the motor industry and a long term vision for the marque. What it initially got was a wealthy entrepreneur with a love of the marque. It was not enough. When Woolf Barnato pulled out, Bentley was successively owned by a couple of big industrial enterprises that knew little of the car business. History shows that neither was a good steward.

For well over half a century, the Bentley name suffered from benign or wilful neglect. The astonishing aspect, though, is that, unlike most of its rivals, Bentley did not die. Its spirit, under-pinned by a wonderful racing record and memories of the glamorous Bentley Boys in the 1920s, was too powerful to suppress. Volkswagen clearly thought the marque retained something of value when it committed nearly $1.7bn/£1bn to a proper Bentley revival at the end of the 20th century.

Given its unhappy history, though, it is hard to believe Bentley did not lose something along the way. This book is an attempt to establish how faithfully the DNA of today's Bentleys reflects that of the cars created by the founder. The journey of discovery turned into a turbulent ride.

Richard Feast
Winchelsea, England *May 2004*

"It was an anxious moment for everyone involved in the creation of the first all-new, dedicated Bentley in seven decades. For the first time, they were about to get some dispassionate assessments of the car from outsiders"

Chapter 1

The legend lives again

A series of well-maintained A-roads snakes along the coast of the northern Scottish mainland. The gentle dairy farming country of the east gradually eases into the gaunt, grey mountains and sparkling sea lochs of western Sutherland, one of Britain's wildest and most magnificent regions. On a sunny July morning, the majesty of this barren landscape is breathtaking. Outside the few towns that dot the route, sheep outnumber people even at the height of the holiday season. There are occasional delivery vehicles and tourist cars, even a few hardy cyclists, but for anyone with a fast car, this remote region provides some of the finest driving country in the world. Bentley Motors chose entirely the right terrain to show off its new Continental GT in the summer of 2003.

The model was one of the prime talking points among car enthusiasts after making its debut at the Paris motor show the previous autumn.

The shape of the car spoke for itself, and the technical specification and performance claims looked good. But up to that time, no one outside the company had been allowed to drive the car. Now a select handful of journalists from around the globe – a mere 40 – were being let loose with the vehicle. It was an anxious moment for everyone involved in the creation of the first all-new, dedicated Bentley in seven decades. For the first time, they were about to get some dispassionate assessments of the car from outsiders.

An indication of the importance of the occasion could be gauged by the reception for the test drivers. They were met at Wick's desolate airport by a trio of classic R-type Continentals from the 1950s and one of the notorious $4^{1}/_{2}$-litre supercharged Bentleys built in 1930 for wealthy racing car

Move over: the new Continental GT is shadowed by the car that inspired it, the Continental R-type coupe of half a century earlier.

owner/driver Sir Henry 'Tim' Birkin. They were then waved off the following morning from Ackergill Tower, a classy private hotel that hugs the shore just north of Wick, by Bentley's heaviest hitters, each anxious to explain the new car and the revival of the company. The message could not have been clearer: this is what we were and this is where we're going. The coveted DNA of Bentley was coming under close scrutiny by a highly influential group of automotive editors and writers.

There was a broad strategy review by Dr Franz-Josef Paefgen, the top Volkswagen group engineer who became chairman of Bentley in March 2002. The car's technical aspects were outlined by Dr Ulrich Eichhorn, another Volkswagen high-flyer who was the Bentley board member responsible for engineering. Board member Adrian Hallmark, a former chief executive of Porsche GB, spoke about the sales and marketing plans for the car. Doug Dickson, the board member responsible for manufacturing, was once a factory manager at Rover when it was owned by BMW. He told of the revolution that had taken place inside the Bentley factory in Crewe.

Ancient and modern: The exterior design of the Continental GT (above) is a modern interpretation of a much-loved 1950s theme. For the interior (opposite), the parent group's product strategy committee wanted something really sumptuous. It rejected a proposal to give the car a simpler interior more like the old Continental R-type.

Germany's Volkswagen group paid Vickers, the British engineering group, $775 million/£470 million for the famous old luxury car marque in 1998. At the same time, ownership of Vickers' Rolls-Royce brand passed to BMW, which in early 2003 introduced the all-new Phantom. The new owners of Bentley then invested another $800 million/£500 million to jump-start tiny, cash-starved Bentley. To Volkswagen, that level of investment was almost loose change, the sort of money it might spend each year on information technology. To Bentley, it was untold riches. Probably for the first time in the company's history, it had the necessary finances, technical resources and manpower to do the job properly. There could therefore be no excuses.

As the Continental GTs burbled away from Ackergill, these men, and the 3,000 people who worked for Bentley, knew their professional expertise was on trial. What the Bentley executives also knew was that there was a definite change of atmosphere at the parent Volkswagen group. It was not for the better. The money pipeline from Germany was not flowing quite as freely as it had. Besides, getting Bentley to that point had already cost Volkswagen nearly $1.6 billion/£1 billion. It was time, Volkswagen's senior people were saying, that the company began to pay its way.

Bentley was acquired during the heady days of high-spending expansion under Volkswagen chairman Dr Ferdinand Piëch. In addition to Bentley, Volkswagen bought Lamborghini and Bugatti in Italy, created upmarket models like the Phaeton limousine and Touareg sport-utility to rival the best from BMW and Mercedes-Benz, and doubled the size of the group through a global sales push. However, Piëch's vision of platform consolidation left Seats and Skodas looking rather like Volkswagens for less money. At the same time,

These you have loved: A trio of Continental R-type coupes of the 1950s and Old No.2 – a supercharged 4^1/$_2$-litre Birkin car of 1930 – were reminders of Bentley's heritage at the 2003 press launch of the Continental GT.

Mission accomplished: The target for the GT and the R was to create the world's fastest four-seater of its day

Volkswagen failed to produce models for dramatic new market niches typified by the Renault Scenic compact multi-purpose vehicle (MPV) and Toyota RAV4 sport-utility. Neither was Volkswagen's high cost base successfully addressed.

Piëch had retired by the time of the Continental GT launch, replaced by Dr Bernd Pischetsrieder, the former chairman of BMW. His arrival coincided with a general slowdown in car demand in Europe. Coming after several years of record or near-record sales, it began to have an effect on all volume car makers. Volkswagen was no exception. Falling sales and profits required Pischetsrieder to address the group's cost base, and to reconsider some of the product excesses of the past.

It was the sort of thinking that filters through to all areas of the company, and high-profile prestige marques are no exception. The launch of the four-door version of the Bentley Continental GT would go ahead as planned for early 2005, but the proposed convertible version was put on hold for the time being. The new priority was for Bentley to start generating some income, not to suck more money from the Volkswagen coffers. Unfortunately, the

Continental GT was initially slow to do that because of delays to the start of volume production.

Despite those early setbacks, though, the overall outlook was much more positive. By the time the first cars were delivered to customers a few months later than promised, Bentley had well over 3,000 advance orders for the Continental GT, or enough to keep Crewe busy for the whole of 2004. Bentley even appeared to have satisfied those most passionate *aficionados* of the marque, the members of the Bentley Drivers' Club. As chairman of the club, James D. Medcalf is the guardian of the spirit of Bentley. He is also the owner of half a dozen examples, so he knows his Bentleys. 'By and large, they have captured the spirit of Bentley,' he said at the time. 'I think W.O. would have been proud to have his name on it,' he added in a reference to the late Walter Owen Bentley, the founder of the company. Volkswagen could have hoped for no better endorsement.

Other plaudits came thick and fast from the car critics. As editor-in-chief of *Road & Track*, one of the America's most important motoring magazines, Thos. L. Bryant is an experienced observer of the whole business. He said:

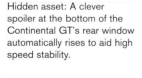

Hidden asset: A clever spoiler at the bottom of the Continental GT's rear window automatically rises to aid high speed stability.

In its element: The prodigious performance of the Continental GT can really be appreciated on open country roads when there is little traffic around.

'I do feel that Bentley has produced an excellent car that carries on the heritage of Bentley – a good, fast car with exclusivity. In the 21st century, I don't think anyone can truly expect an automobile to be "pure" Bentley or whatever, so the Volkswagen W12 engine beneath the hood (bonnet) doesn't detract at all. And the styling, especially the interior, is absolutely first-rate and worthy of the marque.'

Ray Hutton, motoring contributor to the London *Sunday Times* and president of the European Car of the Year jury, was impressed by the Continental GT, though he raised some issues which might offend Bentley purists. 'On the face of it, today's Bentley is truer to the principles established by W.O. Bentley than at any time in the past 50 years. The Continental GT is, like the 1920s Bentleys, a hefty, powerful sporting car. And Bentley has won Le Mans again. W.O. would be proud – or would he?', Hutton wondered.

'If Bentleys as badge-engineered Rolls-Royces were – as enthusiasts believed – an insult to the marque, what are we to make of something that is a Volkswagen Phaeton in fancy dress? A Volkswagen. From Germany. Designed by a man from Skoda. More likely that W.O. is spinning in his grave, bemused by the way the motor business has turned out.

'That said, I think the Continental GT is exactly the right vehicle for Volkswagen to relaunch Bentley. It looks good, is beautifully made and furnished, and is cleverly priced for the rich to buy without too much thought or feelings of guilt. And it distances the new Bentley from BMW's Rolls-Royce.'

So car buyers, members of the Bentley club and the media seemed unanimous in their praise for the Continental GT. But for a product whose mission was to recreate some of the Bentley mystique of the past, it had to pass an appraisal by the professionals of the design world. That came towards the end of 2003, when the Continental GT was awarded the title of *L'Automobile più Bella del Mondo* (the most beautiful car in the world). The title was made in recognition of 'the development of formal continuity and excellence of workmanship' shown by the Continental GT.

Dirk van Braeckel, the design director of Bentley, was particularly pleased that the award was made by organisers in Italy, a country with an unequalled reputation for style and elegance. He added: 'It is a very important award for us, as the most critical consideration in the styling of the car was that it should not only be forward looking but also utterly faithful to our heritage. This design award is further evidence that we have succeeded in that aim.'

The Continental GT, then, is generally accepted as a sympathetic, modern interpretation of a marque born more than eight decades earlier. Bentley's design and production plan represented an astonishing achievement

"If Bentleys as badge-engineered Rolls-Royces were – as enthusiasts believed – an insult to the marque, what are we to make of something that is a Volkswagen Phaeton in fancy dress?"

Style statement: Whatever else changed, the winged B badge has been a prominent design feature on Bentleys from the start of the company.

The way ahead: The radiator grille may be shallower, but the Bentley heritage is unmistakeable. The Continental GT's paired headlights, which echo the look of earlier cars, are to become a design cue on future Bentleys.

considering what happened to the car industry, and to the world in which it operated, in the intervening years.

The business of designing, engineering and manufacturing cars was turned upside down by the creation of new technologies and materials, and by the invention of electronics, which control everything from early concept sketches and crash simulations to material flows in the factory and customer ordering systems. By contrast, the engineering of the early Bentleys was essentially that of the horseless carriage era, except that Bentley dispensed with the horses.

More recently, the car industry was part of the inexorable rise of marketing. Unlike engineers, whose lives are ruled by the laws of mathematics, physics and chemistry, marketing campaigns are based on nuances, on the dreams, perceptions, aspirations and images that a company thinks would appeal most to potential buyers. The days when one man's intuition dictated the size, the shape and the specification of a car, as it did in W.O.'s day, have been replaced by market research, car clinics and focus groups. It is little wonder that many current cars are so unmemorable.

Geo-political shifts also changed the world in which car makers operate. The steady elimination of many trade barriers, greatly improved transport links, and the triumph of free markets over centrally planned economies contributed towards a series of international mergers and acquisitions. Small companies were bought by bigger companies, or allowed to wither. In the current global, post-national world, yesterday's enemies are today's allies. Tiny Bentley is part of a giant German industrial group. The cars are still assembled in the UK, but their engineering building blocks are created in Germany. The head of Bentley design is a Belgian who previously worked for

Master of disguise: The Continental GT shares much of its technology with the Volkswagen Phaeton limousine. Car critics cavilled, but few buyers seemed to notice.

Skoda in the Czech Republic. Such is the international nature of the business now that the man who designed the exterior of the Continental GT is a young Brazilian who saw his first Bentley when he arrived in England.

It is possible – probable even – that W.O. Bentley would not have liked the world today, or the car business. He was a product of an era when the country where he was born was a global powerhouse. The defiant and oak-like character of the cars he built – patriotic ripostes to all those fancy foreign firms – reflected that. Commercially, though, Bentley's fledgling enterprise was a failure, just as his country's indigenous motor industry ultimately was. As an independent company, Bentley sold cars for only a decade before its owner was forced to call in the receivers. The four-decade period of control by Rolls-Royce, one of Bentley's big rivals, could at best be characterised as one of indifference. The services of Bentley (the man) were dispensed with, and Bentley (the marque) almost died. Vickers' more recent stewardship of

Two of a kind: The Continental R-type coupe (foreground) was a trend-setter in its day. Shortly after seeing one for the first time, the designer of the Continental GT came up with his first sketch for the car in the background.

Bentley and the car-making side of Rolls-Royce was little better. While the potential of the Bentley brand was latterly recognised, it was never supported with appropriate levels of investment. That came only after the the take-over by Volkswagen.

The only things in common between W.O.'s original 3-litre of 1919 and the latest Continental GT are the name and the winged-B badge. And yet, despite all the changes and the long periods in the wilderness, the spirit of Bentley refused to disappear. Indeed, the appeal of its heritage was powerful enough to persuade Volkswagen to part with nearly $1.6 billion/£1 billion in order to revive the brand properly. Today when Bentley Motors executives sit down for a meal together, they have taken to toasting the memory of 'W.O.' It is a fitting tribute. W.O. Bentley, who died in 1971, may have forfeited his company all those years ago, but he clearly created something very special.

"W.O.'s passion for steam power was overtaken by a fascination with the internal combustion engine, whose development in cars and motorcycles was gathering pace"

Chapter 2

How the legend was born

T he original Bentley Motors was the most unlikely creation of Walter Owen Bentley, who was born on September 16, 1888. He was brought up in comfortable surroundings in north London in a gentle era of horse-drawn cabs. He was, he later acknowledged, generally spoiled by his eight older brothers and sisters, whose family nickname for him was The Bun, on account of his dark eyes and slightly chunky physique. Formal schooling, initially at England's exclusive Lambrook and Clifton schools, appeared to hold little appeal for young Walter, though he developed a love of cricket that gave him more pure pleasure 'than anything else in life'.

From an early age, W.O.'s other fascination involved mechanical objects in general, and steam trains in particular. It was little surprise, then, that in 1904 he became a premium apprentice with the Great Northern Railway at Doncaster in the north of England, where his middle-class southern accent contrasted with the earthier tones of the regular apprentices. While there, W.O.'s passion for steam power was overtaken by a fascination with the internal combustion engine, whose development in cars and motorcycles was gathering pace. He took up motorcycling and, when his apprenticeship was completed six years later, decided to make a career in the burgeoning car business. W.O. moved to London and spent a couple of years at the National Cab Company in Hammersmith, before going into partnership with his brother, Henry, to sell French-made DFP cars from premises in New Street Mews, just off Baker Street.

The routine was set. W.O. sold DFPs during the week and raced them at the Brooklands track and at the Aston Clinton and Shelsley Walsh hill-climbs

Proud father: Company founder W.O. and (at the wheel) George Duller, one of the famous Bentley Boys, in 1927.

How it began: The privately entered 3-litre of Duff/Clement finished fourth in the opening Le Mans race of 1923. They won the following year. Note the challenging track conditions.

Quick start: A few months after creating his company, W.O. was at the wheel of his prototype Bentley, referred to as EXP1.

at weekends. He was quite successful, especially after secretly commissioning some aluminium alloy pistons for the cars. It was unknown technology in an era when pistons were invariably made of light steel or cast iron. The performance gains with aluminium were notable, though W.O. cannily kept the secret to himself. The success of the experiment had a profound influence on his thinking for the rest of his life.

When the Great War broke out in 1914, W.O. joined the Royal Navy Air Service, where he designed the air-cooled rotary aircraft engines known as BR1 and BR2 (Bentley Rotary) that powered Sopwith Camels. Naturally, the engines used aluminium alloy pistons. W.O. also convinced Rolls-Royce to use the material for the pistons of the Eagle aircraft engine it then had under development.

The success of the Camel fighter, and the performance and reliability of its engine, gave W.O. a great deal of quiet satisfaction, though it brought him no significant financial reward. But W.O. made a handsome contribution to his country's war effort, and his standing as an engineer was widely recognised by his peers. On a personal level, though, he was dealt an appalling blow. W.O. was developing his career in the motor business when Leonie, whom he

> "Without that success in motor sport, there seems little doubt that Bentley would today be a footnote in the history books, as dead as Darracq or Duesenberg "

had married on New Year's Day 1914, died in the great Spanish Flu epidemic of 1918. They had been married for less than five years, much of which was spent apart because of W.O.'s war work.

After the upheaval of the war and the traumatic loss of his wife, W.O. clearly needed a new focus in his life. The setbacks allowed him to funnel all his energies and ideas into setting up his own car-manufacturing business. The design of the first chassis and engine was undertaken in offices in Conduit Street in London's affluent Mayfair district, and construction took place in New Street Mews, to the displeasure of local residents. The prototype of Bentley's first car, the four-cylinder 3-litre, was completed in 1919, but a couple of years elapsed before production cars were ready for delivery to the company's customers.

Starting a car company from scratch represented a superhuman effort because, with no established supplier network, every component had to be designed by W.O. and manufactured to the correct specification. Bentley Motors was constantly under-funded, but, against all the odds, it moved to a proper factory in Cricklewood, north west London, and succeeded in establishing a niche for its high performance cars. Thanks to the determination of W.O, Bentley was off to a solid start.

Good products, though, are merely the foundations of a sound and lasting reputation. It then requires even more investment, unswerving management vision, and a sequence of equally good models over many years to create a legend. Whether that status is then called breeding, heritage, class or DNA, it is generally achieved only by consistently high standards, an awful lot of patience and an ability to charge plenty of money for the products.

In today's car business, Mercedes-Benz and Porsche have had it for years. BMW and Audi acquired it more recently. Alfa Romeo and Cadillac once had it, only to squander it. While Ford and Peugeot have been around long enough to qualify, they don't because so many in the developed world can afford one. Honda and Toyota, desperate for global recognition, have not yet achieved legendary status. And Hyundai and Seat probably never will have it. There are exceptions, even if Lamborghini (founded 1963) is regarded as an *arriviste* company by devotees of Ferrari, which was founded all of 16 years earlier. In much less time than that, though, the puny car company started by W.O. Bentley became a legend in its brief lifetime, and the marque (now with a new lease of life) continued for long afterwards.

And yet, Bentley's beginnings were inauspicious. This is a marque that owes its origins to an engineer who was, thanks to an acknowledged lack of effort on his own part, poorly educated. He learned his craft on mighty steam locomotives in the early 20th century and came to maturity as a designer of engines for the flimsy aeroplanes that fluttered above Flanders fields during the Great War. They were not obvious attributes for running a car company, as events proved only too clearly. The underfunded car company the young man created after the war lasted a scant 12 years before it collapsed in commercial disaster. Even by that stage, ownership of the company that bore his name had passed to one of its wealthy clients. The founder was never comfortable working for the famous firm that bought Bentley's assets, and left at the earliest opportunity. He never returned.

But the Bentley name endured, despite its shaky foundations, the brevity of the early years, a business failure, and often callous neglect by the owners of the marque over the following decades. The real curiosity is that the name today is still one of the world's great automotive icons. Why is that?

The conclusion must be that the Bentley reputation survived the setbacks because what W.O. designed was a series of cars that caught the imagination of the public at the time. Bentleys were fast, effortless and strong. They characterised the need for speed in the 1920s and into the 1930s after Bentley had left the company that carried his name.

Malcolm Campbell, Henry Segrave, Parry Thomas and others battled to be the fastest man on land. In the air, pioneering long-distance flights were front-page headlines, while Supermarine and Rolls-Royce embarked on a successful scheme to win the Schneider Trophy in perpetuity for Britain. Later, the *Queen Mary* and *Normandie* vied to be the fastest liner across the Atlantic Ocean, and Sir Nigel Gresley's *Mallard* steam train thundered across England at an astonishing 126 mph. National pride was a huge element of these various achievements as it was when Bentley went motor racing.

It is one thing to make good cars, but quite another to convince would-be customers. Those were the formative days of the car industry in Britain, with scores of hopeful, and hopeless, fledgling companies desperate to succeed. W.O. had to spread the word about Bentley in competition with formidable companies like Rolls-Royce, Napier, Sunbeam, Lagonda, Daimler, Humber and many more. In an age of speed, there was no time to build that reputation slowly, steadily, surely. W.O. famously wrote in his 1967 book, *My Life and My Cars*: 'To design and build a new motor car in 1919 without substantial capital was like being cast on to a desert island with a penknife and orders to build a house.' The company sank all available money into car development and production, and never had enough left over for a decent advertising campaign that would establish proper public awareness of the name. In that, it was no different from so many other start-up companies, then and now.

And yet, Bentley suddenly became one of the most fashionable names of the 1920s. It happened almost by accident. While W.O. was a keen and active

> **Bentleys were fast, effortless and strong. They characterised the need for speed in the 1920s** ""

The quiet man: W.O. attributed his shyness to an inheritance from his father. He grew up in a large and lively middle class household in north London.

racing driver himself, he considered the challenge of France's then-new 24-hour motor race at Le Mans was too great for a company that had been selling cars for only a couple of years. Initial scepticism was converted into unfettered enthusiasm following a last-minute visit to the first event in 1923. When a privately entered Bentley finished second, there was no turning back for W.O. The company went on to win five of the following seven races. While Bentley had plenty of everyday problems balancing its books, it beat the best that dared venture to Le Mans, including Loraine, Stutz and Mercedes. Without that success in motorsport, there seems little doubt that Bentley would today be a footnote in the history books, as dead as car builders like Darracq or Duesenberg.

Bentley's racing success also became the cornerstone of a motor sport industry in Britain that blossomed even as the country's conventional motor industry withered many years later. In the 1920s, it bought fame to the Bentley company more effectively than any conventional advertising campaign, according to W.O. At a time when a Bentley 8-litre chassis sold for $2,775/£1,850, Bentley's annual motor sports programme cost in the region of $3,750/£2,500 after making allowances for starting and prize money and fuel and oil company bonuses, he later wrote. (If true, that looks like a bargain today. To recover the cost of Team Bentley's 2003 Le Mans win, the company would have had to sell dozens of top model Arnages.) W.O. was convinced the money was well spent because, he reported, the company allocated between two and five times that amount on press advertising even when Bentley was at its peak on the race track.

There was another element that contributed hugely to the enduring Bentley legend. It involved the young daredevils who hurled the cars so successfully round circuits like Le Mans, Montlhéry, Brooklands and the Isle of Man. They became known as the Bentley Boys, a group that epitomised Britain in the Roaring Twenties. It comprised an ad hoc group of amateurs of independent means who wanted to have a good time, on and off the track. They had seen too many friends, cousins and uncles slaughtered in the Great War. The Communist revolution in Russia led to the execution of the Tsar and his family… the old order was under attack. Now there was rising nationalism in Germany, Italy and far-off Japan. Who knew what tragedies would unfold next week?

For most people in Britain, and in the rest of Europe, life was simply a daily struggle for survival, but a certain wealthy stratum of society lived life to the full. W.O. suggested the company's motor racing, and the activities on and off the track of the Bentley Boys who drove them, 'added a touch of colour, of vicarious glamour and excitement, to drab lives'. He was probably right. At a time when many rural folk barely left the villages of their birth, and when the unrelenting grind of poverty, disease and malnutrition sent too many city dwellers to early graves, the Bentley Boys were not half-hearted in their pleasures. In addition to their motor-racing commitments, there were summer holidays in the south of France, shooting parties in Scotland and skiing in Switzerland. In between, there were the parties and dances at London's fashionable Savoy and Claridges hotels, all attended by an endless

> "Bentley's racing success also became the cornerstone of a motor sport industry in Britain that blossomed even as the country's conventional motor industry withered many years later"

Design fault: W.O. Bentley considered the principles of supercharging were flawed. Despite this, the blown 4^1/$_2$-litre Birkin cars came to epitomise Bentley towards the end of its independence.

Test of a Three Litre Bentley

Spreading the news:
The first Bentley road test
appeared in *The Autocar* in
1920, nearly two years before
the first customer took
delivery. Subsequent publicity
for the 3-litre (opposite)
featured then-fashionable
Egyptian-style graphics

succession of pretty girlfriends. Today, the tales of the Bentley Boys read like
a hedonistic existence fed by a surfeit of time and money. It was, perhaps,
a preview to the exuberance of the Swinging Sixties in Britain, played out on
a less egalitarian level.

For those involved, it all seemed too good to be true. It was. Bentley
Motors secured some well-connected customers, but the reality was that its
3-litre model cost more to manufacture than it could be sold for. Additional
models were under development, but they would require still more
investment to take them to market. Towards the end of 1925, only four years
after delivering his first customer car, W.O. was obliged to sound out one of
his wealthy clients about refinancing the company.

The man he talked to perhaps personified the Bentley Boys better than
anyone: Captain Woolf 'Babe' Barnato, racing driver, playboy, an
uncompromising competitor and heir to more money than most people could

decently spend in a lifetime. After Barnato took over Bentley Motors in 1926, he installed some of his own business advisers in the company but retained the services of W.O. as principal engineer and head of the racing department. Motor racing took on an even more significant role within the company after the change of ownership, with Bentley recording four consecutive wins at Le Mans between 1927 and 1930; Barnato himself was at the wheel for three of those wins. The era is remembered as the hey-day of the Bentley Boys. It was also the company's swansong.

Even someone as rich as Barnato was not immune to the effects of the Wall Street Crash in 1929. Demand for all cars quickly vanished, especially for expensive models like Bentleys. Unfortunately for Bentley Motors, the change occurred just as it launched its biggest and most opulent model, the 8-litre. When Bentley Motors became a luxury Barnato could no longer

THE THREE LITRE BENTLEY

TO THE MAJORITY of Motorists a car is a necessity and a means of transit. Without being a technical expert, the purchaser who is interested in the details of a car will be inclined to ask this question : " *Where there are so many first-class makes of car, what are the outstanding features of the Bentley design, and what benefit will I get from them.*" For the 1924 Season, Messrs. Bentley Motors Ltd. are offering the motoring public two distinct models, both fitted with front wheel brakes—the Standard Model and the Speed Model. When the Bentley Cars were first put on the market it was necessary to undertake a considerable amount of racing, both on road and track, in order to convince the motoring world that the cars were strong and reliable. The guarantees with regard to speed, petrol consumption, and material, had to be substantiated, and the idea grew in the public mind that the Bentley Car was designed for the use of speed enthusiasts and the younger generation generally.

For the last year, however, the Company has been building a long-wheelbase model, as the result of considerable demand from customers. This chassis is capable of accommodating coachwork of the limousine and other chauffeur-driven types, and its all-round success in the hands of customers has emboldened the Company to make it the Standard Model for 1924.

The Sporting clientele have not been neglected, and the well-known Short-wheel-base (TT) Model has been brought thoroughly up to date by the fitting of four-wheel brakes and a special Smith-Bentley carburettor. This model still retains its unique guarantees with regard to speed, petrol consumption, and reliability, and will continue, with the latest improvements, to be the criterion of excellence of the motoring connoisseur.

For some considerable time the Company has been fully alive to the desirability, even the necessity, of fitting its cars with front-wheel brakes, but has refrained from doing so owing to the numerous difficulties that have been observed in other systems. These brakes are now fitted as standard on all models, after prolonged test, in the full confidence that they will give every satisfaction, and will maintain the Bentley characteristics of simplicity and freedom from trouble.

5

justify, the company was put into receivership. A purchase by Napier, a former Bentley rival, looked certain until it was outbid at the last minute by an unknown representative of Rolls-Royce.

Rolls-Royce changed everything. The new owners eventually brought out some very fine new Bentleys, but they had nothing to do with W.O., who later went to work for Lagonda. The 1931 change of ownership turned out to be the end of the pure Bentley era. It had not lasted long, but the cars of that period, and the racing drivers who won so often and so elegantly in them, set the tone for what became the Bentley legend.

Stormy weather: Bentleys continued to set the pace in motor racing, but financial failure in 1926 was followed by another five years later. New owners Rolls-Royce were not interested in racing.

"The cars of that period, and the racing drivers who won so often and so elegantly in them, set the tone for what became the Bentley legend"

Wheel of misfortune: Bentley made an indelible and lasting impression through motor racing in the 1920s. However, it did nothing to bring stability to the company, which went bust in 1931

Chapter 3

Vintage years

The publication of Filippo Tommaso Marinetti's Futurist manifesto in 1910 generated an outpouring of abstract art that glorified speed, light, noise and dynamism. The manifesto, published in Paris by *Le Figaro*, came at a time when the motor car was in its infancy. It declared: 'The world's splendour has been enriched by a new beauty; the beauty of speed. A racing motor car, its frame adorned by great pipes like snakes with explosive breath…a roaring motor car which looks as though running on shrapnel, is more beautiful than the *Victory of Samothrace*.' The reference was to the famous winged Greco-Roman sculpture in the Louvre museum in Paris. It is a work of art that, though headless, bears an uncanny resemblance to the *Spirit of Ecstasy* statuette that Rolls-Royce commissioned from Charles Sykes, an eminent sculptor of the time, to adorn the radiator caps of its cars.

Fine words and sentiments, of course, but when Marinetti doodled (he doubtless regarded it as art), the cars, aeroplanes and steam trains he drew to represent that speed were anything but futuristic. Less than a century later, it is evident that the speed element of Marinetti's vision of the future was deeply rooted in the present. What he depicted were representational sketches of racing cars of the moment, not the future. The barrel-like bonnet and abbreviated driving compartment of one resembles a steam locomotive of the era. Another has its exposed wire wheels thrust forward, a huge bonnet and a doughty driver barely in control of the monster. That was the way fast cars were then. Consciously or not, that was inevitably the type of car W.O. Bentley had in mind when he set about designing his first car.

Flying the flag: Memories of Vintage Bentleys were kept alive after World War II through race meetings like this (left) at Silverstone organised by the Bentley Drivers' Club.

Speed merchant: The early 20th century drawings of F.T. Marinetti, the founder of Futurism, display a fascination for fast cars (above).

The Bentley 3-litre, developed as EXP1, first burst into life in London's New Street Mews in October 1919. While the cacophony from its four-cylinder engine was like a symphony to its creator, for no silencers were fitted to the exhaust system, local residents were less enamoured. The matron of a nearby nursing home complained about the racket because one of her patients was ill, only to be told, W.O. later wrote in an unnecessarily flippant aside: 'What was the illness of one man? In here, the birth of a new engine was taking place. A happy sound to die by…'

The development 3-litre had the look of the moment. Its front beam axle, suspended on semi-elliptic leaf springs, put the front wheels well ahead of the radiator. The long bonnet was flanked by elongated cycle wings and topped by a shallow, flat windscreen. The open-top, four-seater bodywork was rounded out by a rear-mounted spare wheel. The spare was usually mounted on the side in subsequent models.

The feature of the car that was to set the tone of most later Bentleys, though, was the large, chromium-plated radiator with its V-shape profile and elegantly rounded shell. The winged-B company badge adopted by Bentley was mounted on the top. Both the radiator and the winged-B badge were the work of F. Gordon Crosby, an artist whose work was well known in *The Autocar* magazine. Flanked by a pair of sizeable headlights with chrome surrounds, the look came to epitomise Bentley for many decades. It survived the change of ownership in 1931, the Derby era of Bentley production and the early years in Crewe, only to disappear with the adoption of twin headlights in the 1960s and body-coloured radiator grilles in the 1980s.

Under the direction of W.O., the chassis was designed by Frank Burgess, a former designer at Humber, where W.O.'s wartime aircraft engines were manufactured, and by Harry Varley, formerly of Vauxhall, the UK subsidiary of General Motors. Col. Clive Gallop, who flew BR-powered Camels on the Western Front, joined the team to do the detail design work on the first engine. The 3-litre featured the conventional technology of the time, which meant a substantial ladder frame steel chassis, leaf springs all round, and (initially) braking only on the rear wheels. W.O. acknowledged the influence of two particular cars when he designed the 3-litre engine: the 1912 Peugeot and 1914 Mercedes Grand Prix car. The result was a monstrous monobloc that used aluminium alloy pistons, a single overhead camshaft, four valves per cylinder and twin spark ignition. None of this would have been apparent in an effusive road test published by *The Autocar* in January 1920. It lyricised that the car's speed was like that of an animal straining at the leash, and described the landscape leaping at the driver, and the trees flashing past in a blur. It was perhaps not surprising, as the Bentley was conceived to be

"The feature of the car that was to set the tone of most later Bentleys was the large, chromium-plated radiator with its vee shape profile and elegantly radiused shell "

Big is better: When W.O. decided a Bentley engine needed more power, the obvious answer was to increase capacity or add cylinders. Thermal efficiency was not a consideration.

Nightmare: F. Gordon Crosby's painting for *The Autocar* captures the drama of the notorious 1927 Le Mans crash at White House that claimed five cars. Benjafield and Davis picked their way through the wreckage to win in a 3-litre.

Action replay: Nostalgia for Bentley's great motor racing era in the 1920s is as strong as ever today.

capable of more than 70mph, or twice the speed of most popular models then. Mysteriously, the test neglected to mention any of the car's technical features, prices or availability. In fact, Bentley Motors did not deliver a car to a customer for 20 months. It was to a successful businessman, Noel van Raalte, who had all the right society connections to spread the word about the new marque. W.O. prudently offered van Raalte, who became a regular Bentley customer, a five-year warranty with the car.

By present standards, though, the whole timetable for transforming the concept of the 3-litre from drawing board to reality seems scarcely believable. Between January 1919 and September 1921, the company managed to design, build and develop three experimental models, win its first motor race, exhibit at the London Olympia motor show, create and equip a new factory in Cricklewood, north west London, to assemble production models, recruit a staff to do the job and deliver a car to its first customer. It did so with scarcely any funds, and the absence of any income from finished vehicles during that time. Compared with now, the nature of cars then was relatively crude, but that has to be balanced against the absence of a sophisticated component supplier network. Replicating the endeavour today would be impossible. Well over five years elapsed, for example, between Volkswagen buying the Bentley brand in the summer of 1998 and the first Continental GT going on sale towards the end of 2003. And that was with proper funding and a modern industrial infrastructure in place.

The original Bentley enterprise would probably not have been possible but for the fact that the Bentley brothers still held the import concession for DFPs. While they sold the rights shortly before the company in France went

The way we were: The talent of the artist, F. Gordon Crosby, could take readers of *The Autocar* into the action at Brooklands before the war.

out of business, much of the money that went into the establishment of Bentley as a vehicle maker in its own right came from the profits made on the sale of DFPs in the post-war boom. As the whole Bentley episode was later to prove, it was clearly easier to make money out of selling cars (or anything else for that matter) than manufacturing them. The lesson is as true today as it was then.

The 3-litre went on to become the mainstay of Bentley's business as an independent company. Unfortunately, as pricey as the model was, it never made any money for Bentley Motors. Other, larger Bentleys were introduced after control of the company passed to Woolf Barnato in 1926, but the 3-litre was in production until nearly the end. Just over 1,600 versions were sold, or over half of Cricklewood's total output of 3,061 chassis.

The practice at the time, of course, was for customers to commission their own bodywork and interior finishes from among dozens of coachbuilders. All those companies have since gone out of business, though their names remain part of the legend of early motoring in Britain. Vanden Plas, which made mainly open-top tourers, was by far the most popular supplier for the 3-litre, accounting for nearly a quarter of all bodies. Gurney Nutting, which produced mainly saloons and fixed head coupés, made nearly 150, while Freestone & Webb, Harrison and Park Ward were each responsible for around 100 cars. Whatever bodywork the chassis carried, though, all were unmistakably Bentleys.

Many body builders in the 1920s employed a method of construction developed in France by Weymann. This novel system allowed the body frame (made of ash) to flex with the chassis, a solution that eliminated much of the rattle, boom and wear found on traditional rigid body frames. In the Weymann method, the components were joined by flexible steel strips that held the wooden members slightly apart. Instead of aluminium panels, the frame was covered by a colour-impregnated fabric made of jute and cotton. The interior components were bolted directly to the chassis. The other big advantage, especially important for a performance car maker like Bentley, was to reduce weight.

However, in spite of the benefits of Weymann bodywork, the speed and refinement limitations of the big four-cylinder 3-litre quickly became apparent to W.O. The engines were powerful enough for the open-top sports cars W.O. had in mind, but when buyers specified large, heavy touring bodywork, as many did, it proved a serious handicap to the car's performance on the open road. Despite the fragile nature of the business, Bentley Motors therefore had a six-cylinder $4^{1}/_{4}$-litre model under development by 1924. As part of the testing process, W.O. and a gang of his pals took the car, disguised by a large Freestone & Webb touring body, to watch the French Grand Prix at Lyons. The return journey produced a chance encounter on a *route nationale* with a prototype from another company testing in France: the Rolls-Royce Phantom, which was to go on sale the following year with a 7.7-litre six-cylinder engine.

Each side quickly recognised the opposition. Rolls-Royce, founded in 1904, was widely acknowledged as the maker of 'the best car in the world'. It was the grand old lady of the top quality car market, and the Phantom was its uncompromising attempt to ensure it retained the title. Bentley, which sold its first car less than three years earlier, was the upstart maker of sports cars that recognised the sales (and profit) potential in the type of cars Rolls-Royce was making. The six-cylinder was its bid for a slice of Rolls-Royce's business.

As soon as the Bentley and Rolls-Royce became involved in an impromptu race across the empty countryside of France, it was evident to W.O. that he would have to rethink his plans. His new car was not fast enough. It was not disgraced, but Bentleys were performance cars, and this one was unable to

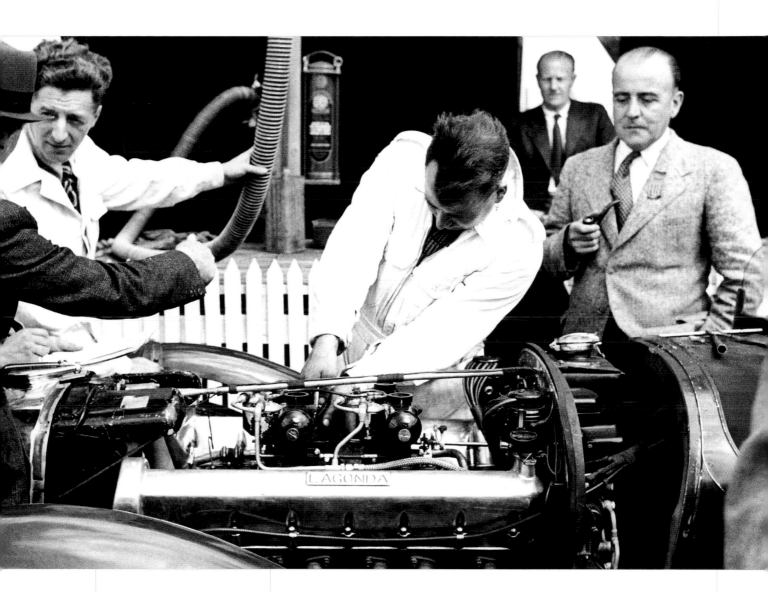

End of an era: W.O. Bentley left Rolls-Royce in 1935 to join Lagonda. With ever-ready pipe, he oversees work on his V12 Lagonda at Le Mans in 1939. The world descended into chaos a few months later.

outperform a stately limousine. W.O. also suspected that, for similar reasons, Rolls-Royce would increase the output of its Phantom as a result of the encounter. Bentley's response was to put its first six-cylinder on sale in 1926, with a displacement of 6.6 litres.

This was the legendary 6½-litre, altogether smoother, quieter and more powerful, though some customers missed the mighty thump of the four-cylinder. The engine enabled a customer to commission almost any bodywork, however heavy or ungainly, without being embarrassed by the

Off to the races: Some of the Bentley Boys line up with their toys. From left to right, Frank Clement, S.C.H. "Sammy" Davis, Dr Dudley Benjafield, Bernard Rubin, Woolf Barnato and Sir Henry "Tim" Birkin, Bt.

car's performance. Like the 3-litres before them, the new cars proved utterly reliable, even in racing. Bentley made 544 $6^{1}/_{2}$-litres between 1926 and 1930. A third of them were the later Speed Six, a model that became W.O.'s favourite. The Speed Six was distinguished by twin carburettors, a performance camshaft and higher compression ratio. Gurney Nutting was the most prolific $6^{1}/_{2}$-litre bodywork supplier (101), though Mulliner was not far behind.

By the mid-1920s, the performance of the 3-litre, a project initiated in 1919, was no longer appropriate for a company that prided itself on the speed of its vehicles. W.O.'s answer was the four-cylinder $4^{1}/_{2}$-litre, which was essentially two-thirds of the six-cylinder $6^{1}/_{2}$; its actual engine displacement was 4.4 litres. The company delivered 667 $4^{1}/_{2}$-litres after its brief debut at the 1927 Le Mans race – an event Bentley was lucky to win after most of its team cars were involved in accidents at the same corner. The $4^{1}/_{2}$ was thus the second most popular Bentley after the 3-litre, which had a lifespan twice as long. Vanden Plas was responsible for 30 per cent of all $4^{1}/_{2}$ bodies, just over 200 in total. Gurney Nutting completed nearly 100 bodies, and Freestone & Webb, Mulliner and Harrison each made 60 to 70 cars.

The $4^{1}/_{2}$ formed the basis of arguably the most controversial of all Cricklewood Bentleys – the famous, or perhaps infamous, Blower Bentleys. The supercharged cars were an unfortunate motor-racing diversion that, according to the founder, played a part in the commercial decline of the company as a whole.

❝To supercharge a Bentley engine was to pervert its design and corrupt its performance❞ – W.O. Bentley

Trouble ahead: The 3-litre of Duller/d'Erlanger at Pontlieu during the early stages of the 1927 Le Mans. The car was eliminated in the notorious White House crash shortly afterwards.

W.O. thoroughly disapproved of supercharging, or forced induction, as an engineering solution to the quest for more power. The founder's simple answer to the need for more power was to make a larger displacement engine. 'To supercharge a Bentley engine was to pervert its design and corrupt its performance,' W.O. wrote 40 years later. The conviction was irrelevant, however. By the time the Blower project was given the go-ahead, W.O. was no longer in charge of Bentley Motors. 'It was the worst thing that could happen to us,' he believed. As things turned out for Bentley, W.O. was vindicated. The Blower cars proved fast but fragile, and never won a major motor race.

The driving force behind the Blower project was Sir Henry 'Tim' Birkin Bt., a wealthy and very successful racing driver who went on to win Le Mans in 1929 (with Woolf Barnato in a Bentley) and in 1931 (with Lord Howe in an Alfa Romeo). Birkin persuaded Barnato to approve the supercharging project, which involved the establishment of a small workshop unit in Welwyn, north of London, in January 1929. Money for the enterprise came from the Hon. Dorothy Paget, who was a wealthy admirer of Birkin.

Five high: Bentley's fifth Le Mans win came in 1930 courtesy of Kidston and Barnato in a Speed Six. They are joined by runners-up Watney and Clement. Bentley was out of racing a few months later.

Walkover: Bentley completed a hat trick with the 1929 Le Mans. The cars were almost unchallenged and filled the first four places.

The chassis and drivelines were supplied by Bentley Motors, and the development work and installation of the Roots-type supercharging were completed in Welwyn by Amherst Villiers.

However, in order for the supercharged cars to be eligible for Le Mans in 1930, Bentley was required to make 50 identical examples that could be used on public roads. It was a serious strain on a company with shaky finances.

The Birkin/Paget team's supercharged cars failed, as W.O. predicted they would, though the official Bentley team managed to triumph in the face of a serious challenge by Mercedes. The event, won by Barnato and Glen Kidston in a Speed Six, was to be the marque's last appearance at Le Mans until the Volkswagen-sponsored return more than 70 years later.

The closest any of the Birkin/Paget Blowers came to success was in the 1930 French Grand Prix at Pau, where Birkin's stripped-down car finished second to a Bugatti driven by Phi-Phi Etancelin. Paget withdrew her financial support for the team at the end of the 1930 season. In a demonstration of the model's speed two years later, though, Birkin set a new record for the Brooklands outer circuit of practically 138 mph. By that time, Bentley Motors had been taken over by Rolls-Royce.

One of the great curiosities of Bentley concerns the iconic status achieved by the supercharged cars over the years. W.O. was convinced the venture played a part in the demise of Bentley Motors in 1931, though he acknowledged the economic meltdown following the 1929 Wall Street Crash was the primary cause. In addition to the financial drain the Blowers imposed on the company, he was philosophically opposed to the engineering principles involved, a belief supported by the failure of the Birkin/Paget cars to put any notable achievements in the motor-racing record books. Only 50 were built, two-thirds of them with tourer bodywork by Vanden Plas.

And yet, those racing Blowers, distinguished by superchargers sticking out of the front between the chassis members, long, louvred bonnets held down by leather straps and little aero windscreens passed into legend. They lacked the racing pedigree and the commercial appeal of the 3-, $4^{1}/2$- and $6^{1}/2$-litre models, and they were regarded with total disdain by the company's founder, but they came to symbolise Bentley at that time. Later, the Blowers acquired places in the hearts of car-mad children everywhere when Lesney brought out a Matchbox toy version and Airfix began selling plastic model kits. They, too, contributed to the Bentley myth.

The 8-litre, considered by many marque enthusiasts to be the ultimate Bentley, appeared towards the end of 1930. The model was a natural extension of W.O.'s design philosophy, formed in the locomotive sheds of Doncaster: if you need more power, build a bigger engine. The concept of

> " It was not a good time to sell extravagant motor cars, as even the wealthy Wolf Barnato, the owner of Bentley, later concluded "

Trouble ahead: Clement took an immediate lead at the 1927 Le Mans with Bentley's secret weapon, the then-new 4¹/². When the car was eliminated in the White House crash, victory went to the 3-litre of Benjafield/Davis (No.3).

creating an engine with greater thermal efficiency, of lightening, tuning and refining a smaller unit to produce a higher output (and use less fuel), had no part in Bentley engineering thinking in the 1920s.

The monster six-cylinder 8-litre was the company's answer to the Rolls-Royce Phantom II announced the previous year. The timing of the 8-litre introduction was unfortunate. The economic collapse that followed the crash of the New York Stock Exchange in October 1929 brought business ruin, unemployment and a prolonged depression around the world. It was not a good time to sell extravagant motor cars, as even the wealthy Woolf Barnato, the owner of Bentley, later concluded.

Provocatively, Bentley decided to give the 8-litre a higher price than the Phantom II. It also made the car a bit faster, and decided it had to equal the refinement of the Rolls-Royce. Bentley achieved this by making the 8-litre an enlarged version of the Speed Six, but with a lower chassis, new rear springs

and a different type of gearbox. It was quiet, even more refined than its predecessors and very fast for its time. The 8-litre was said to be capable of 100mph even with a heavy saloon body and full complement of passengers and their luggage. Of the 100 eventually made, nearly a quarter were delivered to Mulliner for bodywork. Thrupp & Maberly, Gurney Nutting and Freestone & Webb were each responsible for another 13.

The 8-litre chassis also served as the basis for what became Bentley's least-loved model, the 4-litre. After October 1929, the mood in the motor trade was grim, and Bentley's finances were particularly shaky. The board of Bentley therefore decided that the company needed something to compete with Rolls-Royce's smallest model, the 20/25 introduced in 1929. To undercut the 20/25 in price, Bentley embarked on the 4-litre, which had to be simpler and cheaper than anything the company had previously produced. For W.O., the proposal to replace his proven formula of an overhead camshaft and four-valve cylinder head design with pushrods that operated two overhead valves per cylinder was a compromise too far. The company was no longer his, but he was still a member of its board – a dissenting member as it turned out. When W.O. elected to have nothing to do with the 4-litre, the company commissioned the engine from Sir Harry Ricardo's well-respected engineering firm.

The boss: Barnato and Birkin celebrate after their 1929 win in a Speed Six. To their right is W.O. Bentley, who by that time had ceded control of the company to Barnato.

The Blower: Tim Birkin, a firm advocate of supercharging, persuaded Barnato to provide some cars for conversion. As W.O. predicted, the supercharged 4½ (above) was not very successful in racing.

W.O. was a dedicated, uncompromising engineer, but not famous for his business acumen. Whatever Ricardo came up with, he would have hated it. No matter that the 4-litre was smooth, quiet and powerful, the technology had nothing in common with anything the company previously did. In the founder's view, it was simply not a Bentley, especially as the engine lacked the marque's characteristic huge reserves of torque. The development was perhaps the equivalent in modern times of the decision to use Ford engines in Jaguars. It was a short-term expedient that may be judged harshly in the long term.

The other problem as far as Bentley customers were concerned was that the 4-litre was installed in the heavy chassis designed for the 8-litre. The finished car's performance was therefore lamentable. Not surprisingly, only 50 4-litres were completed before Bentley Motors was acquired by Rolls-Royce. Mulliner and Freestone & Webb were responsible for about a dozen bodies each.

But Bentley's glory days as an independent were essentially over by the time the 4-litre went on to the market. When Barnato's advisers asked for receivers to be appointed at Bentley Motors in July 1931, the company had been in existence for only a dozen years. In that time, and against phenomenal financial, engineering, manufacturing and organisational odds,

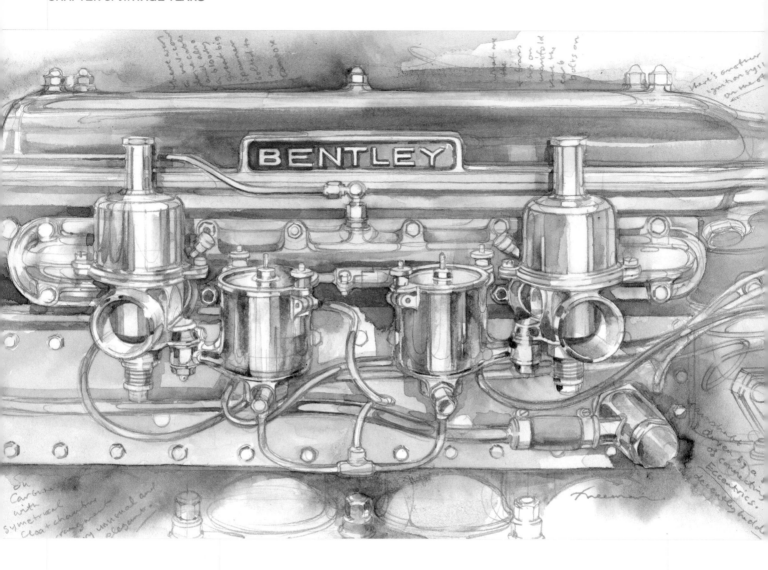

Masterpiece: W.O. Bentley's classic 4¹/₂-litre engine, in a beautiful illustration by the late Bob Freeman. The story of the engine features in MBI's *Legendary Car Engines* by John Simister.

Bentley became world famous. It built some fine cars that were appreciated by the motoring cognoscenti, but that does not fully explain how the Bentley legend was created in such a short time. Other companies in Britain built good cars then, including Aston Martin, Daimler, Humber, Lanchester, Lagonda, Napier, Rolls-Royce and Sunbeam. In other parts of Europe, firms like Benz, Bugatti, Hispano-Suiza, Isotta-Fraschini, Maybach and Mercedes were held in great esteem. Car enthusiasts in the United States, meanwhile, swore by Auburn, Cadillac, Cord, Duesenberg, Packard and Lincoln.

Many of those great names subsequently disappeared, or their reputations were seriously tarnished. Bentley, too, knew its share of uncertainty after the takeover by Rolls-Royce, and then by Volkswagen in the second half of the 20th century. What car buyers never quite forgot, though, were Bentley's racing achievements and the dashing young men who drove them during the 1920s. Neither did they forget the dramatic images they saw of them in their newspapers and magazines. They became part of the emerging Bentley image.

Today, there are plenty of wonderfully atmospheric photographs of Bentley's heroic racing deeds. What the public saw in publications at the time, though, were drawings of the cars at the races – drawings that inadvertently helped to shape the way cars came to look.

> "Bentley Motors pulled out of racing after the 1930 Le Mans, and was out of business a year later"

Communication in the 1920s was unsophisticated. A newspaper or magazine reporter at a motor race considered he was fortunate to get a telephone connection to head office in order to file a story, but a photographer had no chance of getting his work back if the event was held in a remote location. The solution was for an artist to sit at a drawing board in the publication's office and interpret the reporter's story. The artist invariably took a little licence in order to give the illustration more drama.

Dale Harrow, the head of the Royal College of Art's automotive design course, believes those drawings influenced other car designers, even if they were graphically incorrect. 'What the artists came up with were almost artificial reproductions of the racing cars,' he says. 'They had low-slung bodywork, speed lines, exaggerated wheel sizes and clouds of dust to give the impression of speed. The real proportions were completely different, but car designers tended to copy the artistic impressions.'

Life came to imitate art. When a buyer visited a coachbuilder to discuss the bodywork for the chassis he had just ordered, what he wanted was a car that looked like the dashing racing Bentleys drawn by Crosby in *The Autocar*, not something sterile like those that illustrated a company's sales brochures.

Bentley's five Le Mans wins in seven years, then, did more than create the legend. The motor-racing programme indirectly influenced the types of cars customers bought. The first Le Mans win came in 1924 thanks to amateur racer and adventurer John Duff and Frank Clement, the head of Bentley's experimental department, with a privately entered 3-litre. The following two years proved disastrous for the firm, but, under new ownership, Bentley then recorded four successive victories. Dr Dudley Benjafield and Sammy Davis gallantly won in 1927 with a 3-litre that survived an earlier crash. After that, company owner Woolf Barnato scored a hat-trick, winning with Bernard Rubin in a $4^{1}/_{2}$-litre in 1928, 'Tim' Birkin in a Speed Six in 1929 and Glen Kidston in another Speed Six the following year. These were some of the so-called Bentley Boys, whose hard driving on the track and hard living off it contributed so much to Bentley's reputation for speed, style and fun.

But it was the end of an era. Bentley Motors pulled out of racing after the 1930 Le Mans, and was out of business a year later. The company's new owner had a completely different idea about what a Bentley should be.

"But for Barnato, Bentley would have been out of business by the mid-1920s, well before the famous four consecutive Le Mans wins that laid the foundations of the legend "

Chapter 4

When Barnato bought Bentley

Captain Joel Woolf Barnato, who rescued the ailing Bentley Motors with a refinancing package in May 1926, loved fast cars and motor sport. As the son and heir of Barney Barnato, the poor East End lad who emigrated to South Africa and ended up controlling the Kimberley diamond mines with Cecil Rhodes, he could afford to indulge his whim, or any whim for that matter. Whether it was racing cars at Brooklands, powerboating in the south of France, boxing, golf, breeding race horses, or wicketkeeping for Surrey county cricket club, Barnato was the gentleman all-rounder. He was the amateur sportsman who was good at everything.

Barnato was born in London in 1895 and, as befits the son of a wealthy man, educated at Charterhouse and Trinity College, Cambridge. He served as a first lieutenant in the Royal Field Artillery in the Great War, seeing action in Ypres, Gaza and Jordan. When Barney Barnato died in mysterious circumstances on a voyage from South Africa, 'Babe', as he was widely known, became a seriously wealthy young man. It was not long before he took up motor racing and bought his first Bentley. Still in his early 20s, Barnato was part of the high society whirl of post-war London – even if he was Jewish in a period of often-crude anti-Semitism. Barnato relished his ability to be able to throw lavish parties at his country house, Ardenrun, in Surrey a few miles from London, where on one occasion waiters were required to dress in racing-driver suits and helmets. He was also parsimonious, as Piers Brandon, author of an official history of the Royal Automobile Club, noted: 'Barnato was notorious for being one of the richest and stingiest members of the Club'.

Myth-making: Woolf Barnato beat the Blue Train from the south of France to London in one of his Bentleys. There is now some question about whether the car used was this Speed Six coupe portrayed in the famous Crosby illustration.

But for Barnato, though, Bentley would have been out of business by the mid-1920s, well before the famous four consecutive Le Mans wins that laid the foundations of the legend. Without them, who would remember Bentley today? Barnato's money was not just pivotal to the company's rescue. It helped to reduce its reliance on the ageing and unprofitable 3-litre by underwriting the cost of the development and manufacture of the $6\frac{1}{2}$-, $4\frac{1}{2}$- and 8-litre. All were true W.O. designs, but they appeared during the five years when Barnato was in charge of the company. For those reasons alone, Barnato must rank alongside W.O. in forming our current perceptions of Bentley in its glory days.

Then there was Barnato's skill behind the wheel. In W.O.'s judgement, he was 'the best British driver of his day'. The hat-trick at Le Mans is testimony to those abilities. And it was Barnato's lifestyle that personified the group of people the gossip columnists of the day came to know as the Bentley Boys. Despite the name, their reputation owed more to the flamboyant Barnato than to the decidedly dour W.O. Without them both, though, the world today might today be telling tales of the Lagonda Lads or Sunbeam Chasers rather than the Bentley Boys.

By all accounts, Barnato's passion was to excel in whatever he did. He once wagered that his $6\frac{1}{2}$-litre Bentley Speed Six could beat the Blue Train from Cannes on the French Riviera to London. He did so comfortably, in the process earning a reprimand from the RAC, which governed speed events. The car that became known as the Blue Train Bentley had a low, fastback roofline by Gurney Nutting. The restricted rear headroom required a third

Glory days: Three-times Le Mans winner Barnato (right) with fellow Bentley Boys Birkin (at the wheel) and Clement.

passenger to sit sideways, though naturally there was space for a cocktail cabinet. The Blue Train Bentley is still regarded as one of the great seminal models of the era.

W.O. attributed Barnato's success as a racing driver to a keen eye and judgement, courage, discretion and self-discipline. Some measure of that maturity came after Barnato bought Bentley Motors. He was still only 30 and clearly the new company boss. But when Barnato was motor racing, he always deferred to W.O., the team manager, who was seven years his senior. There was a similar arrangement after founder Enzo sold Ferrari to Giovanni Agnelli's Fiat group in 1964: he continued to take all the important motor racing decisions until his death at 90 in 1988.

There were two sides to Barnato. The public knew about the playboy, but anyone who did business with him soon learned about the man's sharp financial acumen. He was perceptive, quick to comprehend and ruthless, an indication that he had inherited his father's business flair. When Barnato agreed to refinance Bentley Motors, the deal re-valued the company's existing £1 ($1.60) shares to one shilling, the equivalent today to 5 pence (8 cents). W.O. had little choice but to agree. There was a certain loss of face, but W.O. was liberated from the constant strain of trying to balance the firm's books

and was able to continue as managing director, at least initially. The change of ownership also held the prospect of a more determined motor-racing programme, which suited the founder and the new owner very well.

W.O. saw the takeover as a calculated gamble on Barnato's part. Barnato was fond of the company, its people and products, but thought the venture could make him some more money, or at least not lose very much. After Bentley was bought by Rolls-Royce, Barnato reported that his five-year period of ownership cost him $145,000/£90,000, equivalent today to around $7.2 million/£4.5 million. At the same time, he admitted to making $190,000/£120,000 on a diamond deal during that period. The two transactions were unrelated – except that they both involved Barnato – but the figures give an insight into the speculative world of the wealthy entrepreneur. Some deals pay, and some don't.

While Barnato was chairman of Bentley Motors, his social commitments and other business interests meant he could devote relatively little time to the company. He therefore appointed some of his trusted business colleagues to the board to oversee day-to-day operations. Less sentimental about the car business, their priorities were to preserve, or add to, the Barnato millions. Some of their decisions – involving the unlamented 4-litre, for example – were not ones that W.O. and his original colleagues would endorse, but they no longer set the agenda by that time. W.O. always considered that Bentley lost a lot of its family, friendly atmosphere in the Barnato period. It may have done. Looking back, it is plain the early days of Bentley Motors lacked commercial understanding. A small, underfunded new enterprise like Bentley needed the business and financial disciplines brought by Barnato's colleagues.

That said, they might not have been as rigorously imposed as was required. Was a major motor racing programme, however little W.O. insisted it cost, a luxury a struggling company could afford? Apart from in 1929, Bentley Motors continued to lose money, though a wealthy man with complex tax affairs like Barnato might have found some nice 'healthy' losses in one of his businesses useful, especially if they contributed to his overall lifestyle. There seems little doubt that Bentley ownership suited Barnato. Even on a simple level, it provided regular motor racing commitments and a plentiful supply of very nice company cars.

Then, in October 1929, came the collapse of the New York Stock Exchange. Investors lost their life savings as millions of dollars were wiped out in a few hours. Banks across the USA closed their doors. Lives and businesses were ruined overnight. The effect was not immediately felt in Europe, but was shortly afterwards when the United States began repatriating overseas money. Only President Roosevelt's New Deal policies in the USA

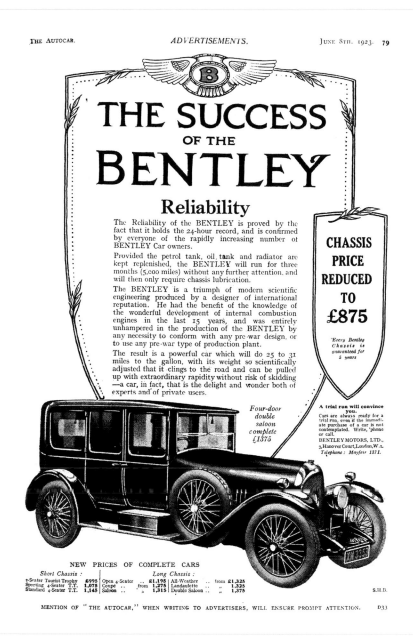

THE SUCCESS
OF THE
BENTLEY

Reliability

The Reliability of the BENTLEY is proved by the fact that it holds the 24-hour record, and is confirmed by everyone of the rapidly increasing number of BENTLEY Car owners.

Provided the petrol tank, oil, tank and radiator are kept replenished, the BENTLEY will run for three months (5,000 miles) without any further attention, and will then only require chassis lubrication.

The BENTLEY is a triumph of modern scientific engineering produced by a designer of international reputation. He had the benefit of the knowledge of the wonderful development of internal combustion engines in the last 15 years, and was entirely unhampered in the production of the BENTLEY by any necessity to conform with any pre-war design, or to use any pre-war type of production plant.

The result is a powerful car which will do 25 to 31 miles to the gallon, with its weight so scientifically adjusted that it clings to the road and can be pulled up with extraordinary rapidity without risk of skidding —a car, in fact, that is the delight and wonder both of experts and of private users.

CHASSIS PRICE REDUCED TO £875

Every Bentley Chassis is guaranteed for 5 years

Four-door double saloon complete £1375

A trial run will convince you.
Cars are always ready for a trial run, even if the immediate purchase of a car is not contemplated. Write, 'phone or call.
BENTLEY MOTORS, LTD.,
3, Hanover Court, London, W.1.
Telephone : Mayfair 1371.

NEW PRICES OF COMPLETE CARS

Short Chassis :		Long Chassis :			
4-Seater Tourist Trophy	£995	Open 4-Seater ..	£1,195	All-Weather .. from	£1,325
Sporting 4-Seater T.T.	1,075	Coupé .. from	1,275	Landaulette .. „	1,325
Standard 4-Seater T.T.	1,145	Saloon .. „	1,315	Double Saloon .. „	1,375

S.H.D.

and the growing arms build-up in some of the big European countries pulled the regions out of the depression.

It was all too late for Bentley Motors. Its biggest, most opulent model, the 8-litre, was already under development when Wall Street crashed. Designed to rival the Rolls-Royce Phantom II, and carrying a higher price, it made its public debut at the London Olympia motor show one year after the Wall Street disaster. The timing could not have been worse, though W.O. believed the only reason the company continued in business for another nine months was because it took 63 orders for the 8-litre. Car production in Britain, which rose steadily throughout the 1920s, dropped 13 per cent within two years of the crash in far-away Wall Street. Even someone as wealthy as Barnato was not immune.

Very grand tourer: Perhaps the most famous Barnato Bentley is the Gurney Nutting-bodied Speed Six coupe, which featured a single transverse seat in the rear. One wonders whether the services of chauffeur Cyril de Heune (pictured) were much called upon.

Royce rivalry: Sir Henry Royce was a co-founder of Rolls-Royce, one of Bentley's well-established competitors. When Barnato pulled out of Bentley, Sir Henry's firm stepped in.

With creditors calling in loans, and unable to pay the weekly wages bill, Bentley Motors was obliged to call in the receivers in July 1931. Barnato told the London *Financial Times*: 'I have personally carried on the company out of my own pocket for the last year, and provided employment directly and indirectly for upwards of 1,500 people.' Even before that, though, Barnato was looking for a way out of Bentley. At the end of 1930, Jack Carruth, a trusted Barnato lieutenant and by then managing director of Bentley, approached Rolls-Royce to suggest the two companies should share sales and servicing and have some manufacturing in common. The threat to Rolls-Royce was that if Bentley went into receivership, a hundred chassis would suddenly be dumped on the market at what was a very difficult period for all prestige car makers.

However, the Rolls-Royce board decided against any investment in Bentley at that time because it was unclear what its liabilities might be. Sensibly, it elected to allow events at Bentley Motors to take their course. If or when Bentley was run by official receivers, Rolls-Royce would have a clearer understanding of the company's true state of affairs.

For his part, W.O. was very excited when he learned about the interest shown in Bentley by D. Napier & Sons, of Acton, west London. Napier was once a well-respected competitor to Bentley and Rolls-Royce, but abandoned car manufacturing in 1925 in order to concentrate on aero engines. Now it wanted to return to the car business. If Napier bought Bentley from the receivers, W.O. could design a new generation of cars. With his BR1 and BR2 experience, he could also aid Napier on aero engine projects. Under the circumstances, it seemed like the best solution. With authorisation from the receiver, Patrick Frére, W.O. started work on a six-cylinder model that was known informally as the Napier-Bentley.

Negotiations between Napier and the receivers continued through the summer and into the autumn of 1931. By November it looked like a done deal. But no one reckoned with the ruthlessness of Rolls-Royce. Napier was already one of Rolls-Royce's big aero engine competitors, and here it was planning to tackle the company head-on once more in the car business. Having rejected Bentley a few months earlier, Rolls-Royce decided it had better buy it rather than let it go to Napier.

Rolls-Royce elected to do so in an oblique way that kept its identity secret. It used a shell company, British Central Equitable Trust, whose representative appeared at the final court hearing in November that was scheduled to transfer the assets of Bentley Motors to Napier. To the shock of everyone, the unknown British Central Equitable Trust representative announced a last-minute counter-bid. The judge, unprepared to act as an auctioneer, suspended proceedings and asked for sealed bids by the afternoon. When they were opened, it was revealed that British Central Equitable Trust was prepared to pay $200,500/£125,275 (about $11.25 million/£6.25 million today), or around $32,000/£20,000 more than Napier.

The true identity of British Central Equitable Trust was not revealed for several days. When it was, it could hardly have been worse news for W.O. Being bought by such a direct competitor would clearly mean the end of the line for the new 8-litre, the big Phantom II rival. It was worse than that, though, much worse.

The Bentley factory in Cricklewood was closed, and the workforce lost its jobs. The founder of Bentley Motors was ordered to return his 8-litre, which he did, and then walked home. W.O., who thought he would simply be able to leave and join Napier, discovered he was part of the assets bought by Rolls-Royce. A subsequent legal action by W.O. and Napier to allow him to leave Rolls-Royce failed. Napier never returned to car making.

W.O., then in his early 40s and with a business failure behind him, had an inauspicious meeting with the co-founder of the world-famous Rolls-Royce car and aero engine company, Sir Henry Royce. Royce, who was knighted the previous year for his firm's engine contributions to the country's Schneider Trophy seaplane win, was 25 years older than Bentley and at the height of his influence. However, he had been in poor health most of his working life, and was to die less then 18 months later.

It was an unsatisfactory encounter, though it had the right ingredients for a meeting of minds. Both men had been railway engineering apprentices, and both had by then gained prodigious knowledge of the aero engine and motor car worlds. Though they were separated by a generation, there ought to have been a lot of common ground. Bentley, it could even be argued, was a natural

You must remember this: The 4^1/$_2$-litre supercharged Bentley became a favourite with post-war schoolboys thanks to toy makers Lesney and Airfix.

The open road: W.O. Bentley designed his cars to be driven far and fast in France and other countries of mainland Europe.

successor to the then-ailing Royce. It was not to be. Royce, seemingly unaware of W.O.'s engineering background, was said to have described him as a 'commercial man'. As the history of Bentley Motors proved, this was one thing W.O. was not.

It was one of the motor industry's great wasted opportunities. W.O., prevented from joining Napier, was initially assigned a nebulous position – 'on not ungenerous terms' – as a liaison officer between the commercial arm of Rolls-Royce in London and the factory in Derby. While he later became a test driver, he was not allowed to be part of the design team for the new car that was to carry his name. That name belonged to Rolls-Royce. Neither was W.O.'s knowledge called on to aid the aero engine side of Rolls-Royce, which was central to Britain's rearmament programme during the 1930s. Instead, W.O. spent his days swanning around Britain and Europe in Rolls-Royces, Derby Bentley test cars, and similar exclusive models made by competitors. It was a comfortable, well-paid job, but it was not what W.O. wanted.

The first Derby Bentley was unveiled in October 1933, six months after the death of Sir Henry Royce and two years after the last Cricklewood Bentley was completed. W.O. continued as a test driver for Rolls-Royce until the middle of 1935, as he was obliged to do under the terms of his contract. Then, in June that year, he was presented with a tricky choice: to renew his five-year contract with his solid and well-respected employer, or to take the offer of another job with a firm whose assets had just been bought from a receiver. That firm, Lagonda, had by a quirk of timing won its first (and only)

> " When W.O. joined Lagonda in the summer of 1935, his links with Bentley Motors and the cars that bore his name were severed for good "

Le Mans 24-hours race a few months earlier, but its future was at best unclear. The new owner, a London lawyer named Alan Good, needed a top-class engineer to design a new generation of Lagondas. The uncertainty of Lagonda was worth it for a man like W.O. In addition to returning to car design and development, it meant liberation from the politics and anxieties of Rolls-Royce. He afterwards recalled that he felt 'quite light-headed with the sense of freedom'.

It was the end of an era. W.O. had lost control of Bentley Motors to Woolf Barnato in 1926, but continued to be responsible for the design and development of its cars. When Rolls-Royce bought Bentley Motors in 1931, though, it acquired the name and elected to ignore W.O.'s engineering talents. When W.O. joined Lagonda in the summer of 1935, his links with Bentley Motors and the cars that bore his name were severed for good.

W.O. Bentley went on to design a number of cars for Lagonda, including a V12 model that finished third at Le Mans in 1939. The famous twin overhead camshaft six-cylinder engine he developed for Lagonda formed the basis of a new generation of Aston Martins after both firms were acquired in the late 1940s by the David Brown Corporation. W.O. Bentley died in a Surrey nursing home on August 13, 1971, aged 82.

The Guv'nor: W.O. Bentley created a motoring legend, even though he was in charge of Bentley Motors for only seven years. He would have been astonished by what happened to Bentley at the end of the 20th century.

Chapter 5

Togetherness: Rolls-Royce/Bentley

The change in direction once Bentley was owned by Rolls-Royce was total. It was a controversial development at the time, and one prone to considerable commercial risk, yet it had a reprise almost seven decades later after Bentley was bought from Vickers by Volkswagen. The central question, then and now, was whether loyal customers who faithfully endorsed the marque for many years would tolerate the radical product changes planned by the new owner.

The Continental GT is only a few months old as this is written and it is too early to judge whether Volkswagen's strategy for Bentley will be a long-term success. In pure number terms, though, the German group can draw some comfort from the sales returns achieved once Bentley was transferred to Rolls-Royce. During Bentley's decade of independence, it achieved an average of just over 300 chassis sales a year. Under Rolls-Royce control in the six years up to the outbreak of World War II, Bentley achieved an annual average of a little over 400 chassis. An increase of one-third over such a short period has to be regarded as a success. On the face of it, then, Rolls-Royce seemed to know what customers wanted better than Bentley did. But did Rolls-Royce make and sell *proper* Bentleys? The issue remains divisive even today.

Immediately after the purchase, there must have been a temptation on the part of Rolls-Royce simply to end Bentley production. As the two marques were after the same wealthy customers, the absence of any Bentleys (together with Napier's decision not to re-enter the car market) would have meant less competition for Rolls-Royce. Thankfully, that was not the course decided on by Rolls-Royce, even if Bentley's two-year absence from the market must at

New direction: Bentley's move to Rolls-Royce at Derby produced elegant models like this Sedanca de Ville designed by A.F. McNeil of Gurney Nutting and built by H.R. Owen.

Derby days: With the move to Rolls-Royce in Derby, Bentleys were turned into "Silent Sports Cars" that featured a variety of bodywork by the top coachbuilders of the day (opposite).

Meanwhile: At a time when Rolls-Royce ownership produced a different type of Bentley, W.O. Bentley busied himself with this V12 for Lagonda (below).

the time have given the impression it was a terminal case. When Bentley did return, it was with a whole new persona. To devotees of the Cricklewood cars, the Derby era models are not true Bentleys. They may not have been in the strict sense of the word, but customers decided it did not matter much.

The Bentleys that W.O. designed and Cricklewood made were replaced by models designed by Sir Henry Royce and manufactured in Derby. Each had different ideas about what a Bentley should be like. The danger of alienating traditional Bentley buyers was exacerbated by Rolls-Royce's decision to suspend the sale of Bentleys for two years. The new owner of the company simply stopped production of one range without having a new one to sell, with all that implied in terms of lost income at a time of increased expenditure. These days, the tactic would appear irresponsible.

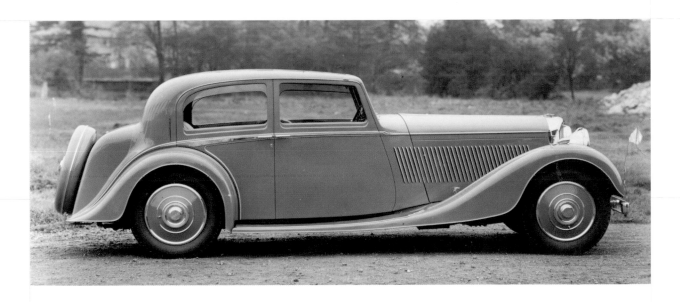

Motor magnate: Henry Royce was a young man (above) when he co-founded Rolls-Royce. By the time his firm bought Bentley, he was world-famous. He died in 1933, two years after the purchase.

Rolls-Royce cast around its engineering department for the first of the models that came to be known as Rolls Bentleys. It started with its experimental Peregrine chassis equipped with a 2.4-litre engine. The Peregrine was a scaled-down version of the Rolls-Royce 20/25 chassis and was, like everything else in the company, designed in minute detail by Royce himself. From the Rolls-Royce perspective, its new Bentley had to be as different as possible from its existing Phantom II and 20/25 models, both of which were introduced a couple of years before the Bentley purchase.

According to William 'Roy' Robotham, who was Rolls-Royce chief development engineer during the transition period, Royce wanted to give the Bentley a higher performance by supercharging the engine. It seemed only natural to Royce. His mind at the time was full of memories of the Schneider Trophy-winning Supermarines with their supercharged Rolls-Royce engines, and he knew other European car companies like Mercedes and Alfa Romeo had successful supercharged models. While W.O. Bentley would have hated the idea, he was not of course consulted. The famous Blower Bentleys developed by the Birkin/Paget racing team became Bentley icons, but W.O. himself vehemently opposed the concept of supercharging his engines. As it turned out, Royce's proposal came to nothing because development testing of the unsupercharged engine in France resulted in persistent big end failures. There was an additional problem procuring suitable Roots-type superchargers.

As uncertainty about the future of Bentley continued, Rolls-Royce's commercial department began to worry that it had nothing to sell to the new acquisition's traditional customers. It was at that time that the development engineers at Derby decided to equip the Peregrine chassis with the 3.7-litre six-cylinder engine from the 20/25. To their surprise, the combination produced a vehicle that had a lively performance, handled very well and had the refinement and silence of a Rolls-Royce. The project was approved in October 1932 by Royce – who died six months later – and launched on the market one year later as the Bentley $3^{1}/_{2}$-litre.

Using an existing Rolls-Royce chassis for the new Bentley meant that the company missed the opportunity to move to independent front suspension, which by the early 1930s was on a number of rival cars. Effectively, Bentley's switch to independent did not happen until after World War II, long after the rest of the industry. The $3^{1}/_{2}$ therefore had semi-elliptic leaf springs all round, just as all previous Bentleys had. In other respects, though, the $3^{1}/_{2}$ was like no other Bentley. Instead of W.O.'s beloved arrangement of an overhead camshaft and four valves per combustion chamber, the $3^{1}/_{2}$ engine used more conventional pushrods to operate single inlet and exhaust valves. Unlike the

"As uncertainty about the future of Bentley continued, Rolls-Royce's commercial department began to worry that it had nothing to sell to the new acquisition's traditional customers"

Lingering legacy: The great coach-building days of the 1930s were largely a memory by the time Franay produced this extravagant convertible Bentley Mk VI in the late 1940s.

Radical departure: The streamlined Embiricos Bentley (above and opposite) looked like no previous Bentley, but it influenced the design of the pre-war Corniche.

engine in the 20/25, which had a carburettor built to Royce's specification, the Rolls Bentley had twin SU carburettors, which gave a significant increase in power. However, the model's very quietness was a concern to the sales department; the $3^{1}/_{2}$ was perhaps too quiet to sell to traditional Bentley buyers, who were unused to such silence and refinement. In the end, Rolls Royce made a virtue of the feature by successfully promoting the $3^{1}/_{2}$ as the Silent Sports Car.

The result was a model that could never have come off the drawing boards of W.O. Bentley, as Robotham explained in reminiscences in the Bentley Drivers' Club's magazine (July 1964): 'To get a true perspective on the part R. (Sir Henry Royce) played in creating the new Bentley it should be remembered that he had designed every part of the new car. All the Derby engineering department had done was to rearrange the components available in a different form to that originally envisaged.'

So, Sir Henry Royce gave Bentley its new direction. The services of W.O. were called on to undertake extensive testing of $3^{1}/_{2}$ prototypes (and Rolls-Royces) in Europe, but that was the extent of his involvement. W.O. professed that he was impressed by the newcomer, but it should not be forgotten that he was employed (on apparently generous terms) by Rolls-Royce up to 1935. The new-style Bentley maintained the high-performance aspect of the old cars, but accompanied it with refinement, comfort and silence. It no longer embraced the more visceral performance characteristics of the vintage cars. An official motor-racing programme was out of the question.

It was a hazardous strategy on Rolls-Royce's part, but one that reflected its complete self-confidence at the time. How could the manufacturer of 'the best car in the world', a company with a burgeoning aero engine business, be wrong? In more modern terms, what Rolls-Royce did with Bentley would be

Age of elegance: The Derby Bentleys came to epitomise the craft of the coachbuilders. This is a 1939 4¼ with saloon bodywork by H.J. Mulliner.

akin to Ford completely changing the character of Jaguar after buying it, or Fiat turning Ferrari into a maker of boulevard cruisers and then pulling out of motor racing. The ideas are unthinkable, yet that is effectively what Rolls-Royce did with Bentley, and with considerable commercial success. Despite the personality change, and despite the disappointment of many owners of Cricklewood cars concerning developments at Bentley under its new owners, the 3½ achieved sales of nearly 1,200 in the four years of its existence. The 4¼, a development of the 3½ launched in 1936, did even better by recording just over 1,200 sales in three years. No Cricklewood Bentley came close to selling rates like those.

In the light of Rolls-Royce's bumper-to-bumper transformation of Bentley, it may be hard today to understand why it was a success. The answers revolve around the great Rolls-Royce company itself. Established three decades earlier, it had built a good sales and distribution network that had all the right contacts among the country's wealthy elite. Buyers were also clearly reassured that a Bentley made by Rolls-Royce was of high quality. In addition, Rolls Bentleys proved to be very effective at high-speed, long-distance cruising of the type then really possible in mainland Europe. It was an appealing combination for anyone with $1,760/£1,100 to spend on a chassis.

But there is another reason. It is the spirit of Bentley, exemplified by that distinctive radiator shell and the huge headlights. Rolls-Royce sensibly relied on the traditional Bentley frontal treatment to nurse the transition from one era to another. The wire mesh grilles of the vintage cars were largely replaced in the 1930s by chromium-plated vertical slats that gave better temperature control, but no one could mistake the Bentley grille.

It was a trademark that successfully carried the Bentley name through an era when car styling in general began to evolve. Many of the open-top vintage Bentleys are reminiscent today of giant green bathtubs on wheels. They are as anachronistic as W.O.'s beloved steam engines in the world of the TGV,

"Rolls-Royce sensibly relied on the traditional Bentley frontal treatment to nurse the transition from one era to another"

France's 180mph train. The technology and materials that went into the original Bentleys, and the way they were made and looked, has nothing in common with modern cars. They had the pugnacious spirit of a bulldog, a devil-may-care personification of a time when the country's imperial reach was still at its height.

By the time the Derby Bentleys began to appear, car design was much more elegant. As the depression caused by the Wall Street Crash faded, colours became brighter and duo-tone paint schemes were seen more frequently. Streamlining, as it was understood then, produced more voluptuous curves. Wings enveloped more of the front wheels, and rear wheel arches often carried spats, all in the name of streamlining and style. Wire wheels with knock-off hubcaps began to be replaced by disc wheels.

The Derby cars were, and remain, some of the most beautiful Bentleys of all time. Park Ward proved a popular coachbuilder during this period, in part because Rolls-Royce took a financial interest in the company in 1933, but Barker, Gurney Nutting, Hooper, Mulliner, Thrupp & Maberly, Vanden Plas, Young and many others produced magnificent cars for their clients. The common theme, the look that cemented Bentley in the public conscious, was invariably the chrome grille and pair of giant headlamps.

Curiously, then, the most famous Derby Bentley of all had nothing visually in common with any of them. It was the 1938 $4\frac{1}{4}$ built for a Greek customer named André Embiricos. The stunning, streamlined Embiricos

Home, James: H.R. Owen built a number of the Sedanca de Villes designed by Gurney Nutting.

The shape of things to come:
Development of the so-called
rationalised range at Derby in
the late 1930s led to the
post-war Bentley Mk VI (left)

" Rolls-Royce's tiny scale as an automotive maker clearly could not justify the continued production of three distinct model lines that had virtually nothing in common "

Bentley, designed by Georges Paulin and built in France by Pourtout Carrossier, had fastback bodywork, a cowl over the radiator and fared-in headlamps in order to improve aerodynamics. Already over a decade old after World War II, the car was raced privately twice in the Le Mans 24-hour race.

The Embiricos car is usually considered to be the inspiration for the experimental Bentley model developed by Rolls-Royce at the end of the 1930s. Known as the Corniche, its design constituted another radical departure for Bentley – and, it has to be said with hindsight, not one for the better. Nevertheless, the Corniche was a pivotal car for Bentley and Rolls-Royce in two important respects.

Rolls-Royce underwent a complete restructuring after Sir Henry Royce died in April 1933. Everything the company did up to that point revolved around the co-founder, whose poor health apparently required him to live and work on the south coast of England during the summer and in the south of France during the winter. So, at a time of primitive communications, the man who made all the important decisions at Rolls-Royce was removed from the commercial side in London and from manufacturing in Derby. It might have suited Royce, but it was a seriously flawed structure for one of the country's leading industrial companies.

The organisation was taken apart as decently as possible after Royce's death. At the same time, a thorough review of the company's strengths and weaknesses was instigated by the newly appointed general manager, Ernest Hives. The report was doubly important because the country's belated rearmament programme relied on Rolls-Royce to produce many of the new aero engines needed by the Royal Air Force. Hives' damning report about a company that had atrophied made ugly reading for Rolls-Royce directors, who authorised the changes required.

The sheer volume of Rolls-Royce aero engine work, which overtook that of the chassis side for the first time in the mid-1930s, masked the lamentable state of the firm's car business. Rolls-Royce's tiny scale as an automotive maker clearly could not justify the continued production of three distinct model lines that had virtually nothing in common. In 1936, those vehicles were the vainglorious Phantom III with its V12 engine, the 25/30 and the Bentley $4^{1}/4$. Rolls-Royce needed component-sharing and economies of scale just as much as mass-producers of cars. The report also highlighted certain quality concerns about Rolls-Royce and Bentley models.

William Robotham, the chassis division's chief engineer, was given responsibility for the development of what was known internally as the rationalised range. Borrowing from American car industry principles, the range was conceived to accommodate three different engines (four, six and

Enemy territory: As Rolls-Royce reshaped Bentley, there was no place for W.O. Bentley. He joined the rival Lagonda company, where he designed its six-cylinder and V12 saloons.

eight cylinders, but with numerous common components) across a standard chassis capable of being made with various wheelbase lengths. Most body styles would be standardised, a task made easier by Rolls-Royce's outright purchase of Park Ward in 1938.

The first Bentley from the rationalised range appeared in 1939 as the Mk V, only 11 of which were completed before the outbreak of World War II. Car-building at Rolls-Royce then went into limbo in order to give priority to aero engines, but the rationalised range provided the modern building blocks to restart chassis production once peace was restored. The two models that became the post-war legacy of that pre-war planning were the Rolls-Royce Silver Wraith and Bentley Mk VI.

Before the war, the series included an experimental high-performance saloon version known as the Bentley Corniche, which was scheduled to go on sale in 1940. The Corniche was the work of Paulin and Rolls-Royce's in-house designer, Ivan Evernden, who departed from traditional Bentley grille practice by using an enclosed, sloping nose flanked by air vents with horizontal bars and fared-in lights. The futuristic four-door cars, which were fabricated by van Vooren in Paris, had fastback lines and fully enclosed rear wheels. Sadly, only photographs exist today. The four Corniches being built or tested were lost in the mêlée of war after Germany occupied France.

The programme was not directly resurrected during Britain's days of austerity after the war, but it served as the basis for what became the classic Continental Type R of 1952. And for that, Evernden reverted to the more familiar and much-treasured Bentley frontal treatment. The Corniche name was later adopted by Rolls-Royce, which made it an unresolved issue when Volkswagen and BMW divided the jewels of the British motor industry in 1998. Will any future Corniche be a Bentley or a Rolls-Royce?

"Although undeniably grand, Bentley had a slightly more egalitarian image than the blatantly elitist Rolls-Royce. Bentley was right for the moment"

Chapter 6

Rolls-Royce loses the plot

Rolls-Royce had a 'good' war. All car chassis production was suspended because of the company's paramount need to produce aero engines for the Royal Air Force and other engines for the Army's military vehicles. Rolls-Royce's first post-war car – a Bentley Mk VI – was not delivered to its owner until September 1946, a full 16 months after VE (Victory in Europe) Day. The Mk VI differed from the pre-war Mk V of the rationalised range largely because it was fitted with a new type of engine, a 4.3-litre six-cylinder monobloc that featured an aluminium alloy cylinder head, overhead inlet valves and side exhaust valves. With the exception of the grille and headlights, there wasn't even a hint of Bentley heritage in the model, though it did not seem to matter.

The Mk VI series did well for the company because Bentley was considered a more appropriate marque with which to return to the car business at the time. Although undeniably grand, Bentley had a slightly more egalitarian image than the blatantly elitist Rolls-Royce. Bentley was right for the moment. That post-war period left Britain having to rebuild its shattered economy and infrastructure. Everything was in short supply, including the good quality steel needed by the company Pressed Steel to build the standardised bodies of the Mk VI. Bread rationing was introduced for the first time. Enormous debt repayments were due to the United States, yet Britain's Labour government embarked on a staggeringly expensive programme of nationalisation, housing construction, social welfare and the establishment of a national health service. The country's Army, Air Force and Navy still had huge commitments around the world, a legacy of the country's imperial past.

Bentley takes wing: Sales of Bentleys far out-numbered those of Rolls-Royce in a period of post-war austerity.

Your carriage awaits:
The Bentley S series was
the height of opulence in the
1950s. Perhaps that's
because it was a Rolls-Royce
by another name.

Britain, the dominant global power at the start of the century, had difficulty adjusting to post-war geopolitical realities.

The war changed Rolls-Royce as well. Its automotive subsidiary, which ticked over during hostilities, was given a new home at Crewe, the factory created at the end of the 1930s to build desperately needed Merlin aero engines. By the early 1950s, Rolls-Royce was an international aero engine maker of great repute and considerable scale, and it also happened to make a few car chassis each year. Rolls-Royce's thinking and decision-making, therefore, were dominated by aero engine specialists. Yet the aero engine sector went through the revolutionary switch from internal combustion engines to gas turbines in the second half of the 1940s. In addition, aero engine projects were so expensive (and strategically critical) that their development costs and purchases were invariably underwritten by government defence departments. The motor industry existed in a much harsher commercial world that, literally, found its customers only when they walked off the streets into car showrooms. And to the aero engine sector, any automotive project was almost loose change by comparison. If the cost of developing a new car was stratospheric, those in the aero engine business were in outer space.

The two sides of Rolls-Royce's business had become inappropriate bedfellows, separated by technology, customers and budgets. Rolls-Royce was in the vanguard of consolidation in the aero engine sector as it bought rival makers de Havilland and Bristol-Siddeley. By the mid-1960s, those

> "The two sides of Rolls-Royce's business had become inappropriate bedfellows, separated by technology, customers and budgets "

Badge engineering: In 1955, the Bentley S series replaced the cars designed before the war. The differences with the Silver Cloud were minimal.

BENTLEY

'S' SERIES

A new motor car representing a logical advance in the design of chassis and coachwork.

Core model: The Bentley Mk VI was Rolls-Royce's main model in the immediate post-war period. Based on a pre-war design, it was sold until 1955.

developments turned Rolls-Royce into the third largest aircraft engine manufacturer in the world after General Electric and Pratt & Whitney, and the largest in Europe.

As all this was happening, the global motor industry was reshaped internally by consolidation and competition, and externally by new technologies and legislation. The effect was to turn little Rolls-Royce into tiny Rolls-Royce. A series of mergers and acquisitions left true power in the car business in the hands of a small number of high-volume groups. The pursuit of scale dictated that to be small was to be vulnerable or sidelined. The prestige cars that only the extremely wealthy could afford during the pioneering era of motoring were eclipsed in Europe (long after America) by the democracy of mass production. New names from Japan – little known in the motor industry before World War II – introduced standards of manufacturing efficiency and product quality that were unrivalled. European and American car makers had to scramble to catch up, prodded from behind by yet more new nameplates from an ambitious South Korea. Along with increasing prosperity, the result was that for the first time an ordinary working family in Europe could afford a car with all the quality and reliability (though not the prestige or longevity) of a Rolls-Royce.

This development raised serious questions about the worth of more expensive brands. Yet there was a determined drive on the part of car makers to achieve higher prestige because it held the promise of higher profits. It

Show over: Any pretence that Bentleys and Rolls-Royces were different was abandoned in the mid-1950s. The Bentley S series (below) was a Rolls-Royce with different badges.

Fashion victim: The third generation Bentley S series featured paired headlights, which were popular in the 1960s. It was not a Bentley design cue from the past.

could be called the trickle-up effect, as Honda and Hyundai went in pursuit of Volvo and Audi, which tried to emulate BMW and Mercedes-Benz, which in turn set out to build more advanced cars than Rolls-Royce. It was soon not difficult for them, because their steadily increasing sales around the world provided them with development budgets that were greater than the turnover of Rolls-Royce.

As a small-scale manufacturer, Rolls-Royce was particularly vulnerable to the arrival of all the electronic controls that revolutionised the way cars are designed, manufactured and equipped. When it eventually recognised it had to buy electronics expertise from German firms like Siemens and Bosch, this most British of car firms went to enormous lengths to keep the development secret. The thought then of a German-owned Rolls-Royce was unimaginable.

Rolls-Royce managed to meet all the new safety, noise and exhaust emissions regulations that emerged from the United States and Europe. Not to have done so would have meant going out of business. But the demands on its time and budgets these caused meant that little Rolls-Royce slipped behind high-volume car companies in terms of technology, build quality and reliability. Rolls-Royce, the custodian of the W.O. Bentley legacy, demonstrably no longer made the best car in the world by the 1970s.

None of these changes seemed to affect the prestige of Rolls-Royce or Bentley, but it did reduce their relative scale and true importance. Rolls-Royce was a giant in the aero engine business but became increasingly irrelevant on its car side. Indeed, its presence in the car business was prolonged only because most of its pre-war competitors went out of business (Bugatti, Duesenberg, Hispano-Suiza, Horch, Isotta-Fraschini and Maybach) or changed direction (Cadillac, Lincoln, Packard). Ferraris and Maseratis were

True to tradition: Convertibles were always a large element of Bentley's history. This is an S3.

> "By default, Rolls-Royce, together with its Bentley marque, inherited a monopoly on the mega-money limousine market"

T for two: A generation later, the Bentley T series was adapted into a two-door convertible that was initially known as the Corniche and later as the Continental.

pricey and exclusive but aimed at a different crowd. Mercedes-Benz and BMW set new technology and quality standards, but the public mistakenly still did not consider them as worthy rivals to Rolls-Royce.

By default, then, Rolls-Royce, together with its Bentley marque, inherited a monopoly on the mega-money limousine market. The company existed as if in an exclusive time capsule. It had no real competition in its select little corner of the car market and its parent company was preoccupied by the aero engine business, in which it was financially cushioned by taxpayers in the UK. It was a state of unreality that could not, and did not, continue.

These factors have to be understood in order to appreciate why Rolls-Royce management failed to look after its car-making side properly. Rolls-Royce exists as a car maker today despite Rolls-Royce the aero engine maker. And with the honourable exception of the Continental R-Type coupé of the 1950s (chapter seven), the pretence that Bentleys were any different from Rolls-Royces had long vanished. The independent Bentley of the 1920s gave way in the 1930s to Bentleys of a different type, but they were at least visually distinguishable from Rolls-Royces. However, the rationalised range

The man who designed Bentleys

John Blatchley was the young designer who created many of the memorable cars made by Gurney Nutting before World War II. Afterwards, he joined Rolls-Royce, where he was responsible for the designs of the Silver Cloud/S series of 1955 and the Silver Shadow/T series of 10 years later.

By that time, Rolls-Royce management was dominated by its aircraft engine business. Cars had almost become a sideline. Believing his contributions were not appreciated, Blatchley abruptly quit in 1969. He was only 56.

His efforts are appreciated by today's car collectors, however. In 2003, the Rolls-Royce Enthusiasts' Club hosted a 90th birthday party for him near his home in Hastings. He is seen above (right) at the party chatting with Simon Taylor, the motor racing commentator and owner of a 1938 Bentley 4 1/4-litre sedanca coupe with bodywork designed by Blatchley when he worked at Gurney Nutting.

Cloud formation: John Blatchley quickly drew this initial sketch in 1951 of the car that was to become the Silver Cloud and S series (above).

Putting in the boot: Blatchley's first job at Rolls-Royce was to give the standard steel saloon – the Bentley Mk VI – a bigger boot. This is his original drawing from 1945 (left).

Junior Bentley: In the immediate post-war years, Rolls-Royce wondered whether buyers would want a four-cylinder Bentley. This is a 1946 Blatchley rendering of what an everyman Bentley might have looked like (right). The car was never made.

Too trendy: The board of Rolls-Royce decided in 1951 that Project 11B VIII (above, in full scale model form at Park Ward) represented too big a styling leap from the then-current Mk VI to be its 1955 replacement. Instead, it selected John Blatchley's rendering (previous page) as the starting point for the new S series and Silver Cloud, which were developed as the Siam.

Siam to Burma: The project to replace the S and Silver Cloud was known as Burma. This radical clay model proposal with full width grille and tail fins (right) was rightly rejected in 1959. Burma eventually became the T series and Silver Shadow in 1965.

The illustrations on pages 94-97 are from John Blatchley's personal archive, which has been bequeathed to the Rolls-Royce club. Sadly, much of the material in the official Rolls-Royce company archives was destroyed during the 1960s.

"Rolls-Royce were hopeless," Blatchley recalled. "They threw everything away. I had detailed quarter-scale drawings of all the cars. They've just been lost. I saved some drawings because I wouldn't put them into the system. I kept them in my own office. I'm glad I did, because they'd all have got burned with the rest of the stuff."

> "The reality was that the tiny scale of Rolls-Royce (including Bentley) as a car maker meant it could barely maintain one brand, let alone two"

Stately progress: If you have a chateau, you obviously need an appropriate carriage to go with it. The Bentley T series, together with its Rolls-Royce equivalent, became the most successful series made at Crewe.

begun before the war and resurrected afterwards signalled the end of Bentley as a separate marque. Until the early 1980s, each successive pair of new products then welded the two more closely together. The process, while initially encouraging for Bentley, went so much in the wrong direction that the marque nearly died as a result. The sales returns tell the tale.

Rolls-Royce sold just more than 7,200 Bentley Mk VIs (including the later R-Type with a larger boot, and stunning Continental coupé) from 1946 to 1955. That was nearly three times as many as the number of mechanically related Silver Wraiths and Silver Dawns sold over a broadly similar period. When the ranges were replaced in 1955 by the Silver Cloud and S series – with barely a badge to distinguish them – Bentleys were initially more popular. However, they accounted for only 47 per cent of all sales by the time the series was replaced a decade later by the Silver Shadow and T Series.

This pair amounted to Crewe's most ambitious car project. They were physically smaller than their predecessors, yet contained greater space for occupants and their luggage. That was attributable to the company's switch from its traditional body-on-frame construction to unitary steel body-chassis units – decades after the rest of the motor industry moved in the same direction. The newcomers featured other specifications that were new to the company, if not to the broader motor industry, including all-independent suspension, four-wheel disc brakes and hydraulic ride height control. Visually, their three-box profiles ensured the cars looked different from any previous Rolls-Royces and Bentleys.

The cars caught the imagination of buyers, who had recently been reminded by Britain's Prime Minister, Harold Macmillan, that they 'had never had it so good'. This was a period of increasing prosperity that led to the Swinging Sixties – a decade of more liberal attitudes and personal indulgence. The Silver Shadow and T Series became the most popular models ever made by Crewe. Just over 32,300 were sold in the 15 years up to 1980. It was good news for the company, but less so for the Bentley brand, whose badges ended up on only 7 per cent of all of them. After benign neglect, oblivion seemed like the next step.

On a micro level, Rolls-Royce these days is accused of not understanding the value of its Bentley asset, of failing to nurture it properly during that period. That's true, but the bigger picture is that Rolls-Royce's aero engine mindset served to marginalise Rolls-Royce as a car maker as well. The reality was that the tiny scale of Rolls-Royce (including Bentley) as a car maker meant it could barely maintain one brand, let alone two. Under the circumstances, the choice at the time must have looked straightforward: Rolls-Royce was the name of the parent company, as well as being much better

Going down: Rolls-Royce scaled back the importance of the Bentley T series in favour of the Silver Shadow. By the end of production, even the Bentley's instruments carried Rolls-Royce badges.

known than Bentley around the world, particularly in the USA, its hugely important export market.

The issue raises questions that are as relevant today as they were then concerning the wisdom of many takeovers. A new owner's well-meaning promises and initial enthusiasm are frequently ground down by the complexities and financial requirements of making it all work. It took Rolls-Royce only a few years to emasculate Bentley in everything but name. From the rationalised range, which was conceived in the late 1930s and launched properly in 1946, to the Silver Shadow/T Series that were in production when Rolls-Royce's world collapsed in 1971, Bentleys were Rolls-Royces by another name. The only exception was the Continental, little more than 200 of which were made.

Name change: The Mulliner
Park Ward-made Bentley
convertible that started life as
the Corniche eventually
became the Continental. Both
names are part of Bentley's
history.

The fundamental problem was that at the highest level within the Rolls-Royce group, no one understood the car business, or the seismic consolidation and technology shifts that were taking place within it. The people running the car division had a better idea – they went to the motor shows and talked about the issues to their peers from other car companies. Their difficulty was that they did not have enough clout to influence the group's major strategic thinking.

Ultimately, it was the Rolls-Royce aero engine scandal in 1971 that resulted in the car division being hived off. At that time, it was believed to be a marginally profitable unit but it accounted for only 5 per cent of the group's business. The car company's subsequent flotation led to what was an ultimately unsatisfactory merger with Vickers, and to the eventual separation of the brands at the end of the century. Only in competition are Bentley and Rolls-Royce once more beginning to assert their individuality.

"The Continental period is a tantalising hint of what Bentley might have become if Rolls-Royce's top management had had the vision, the courage, and the funds to develop the idea"

Chapter 7

Memories are made of this

Brief encounter: The Continental coupes came and all too quickly went in the 1950s. They symbolised the Bentley ethos better than any other model made by Rolls-Royce.

I f the three decades and more that followed the end of World War II were depressing for the Bentley nameplate, one brief episode is still fondly remembered by the marque's devotees, and by car enthusiasts in general. The Continental period is a tantalising hint of what Bentley might have become, given some vision from Rolls-Royce's top management, courage and the funds to develop the idea. As it turned out, the Continental was more like a half-hearted experiment that happened to drag on for nearly a decade. The period produced what history now judges to be the most memorable Bentleys of the era, and some of the best of all time, yet Rolls-Royce decided there was no future for the Continental. It buried the whole idea and the name, which was not resurrected until Rolls-Royce and Bentley had new owners and new managers.

Bentleys from the 1940s onwards – the Mk VI and R, the S and the T – were products of Rolls-Royce badge engineering. In every respect apart from their labels, they were Rolls-Royces. That meant they were wonderful cars, but they had none of the DNA from the W.O. Bentley era, nor even any of the product distinction of the early days under Rolls-Royce. The Continental, though, was the philosophical descendant of those magnificent Derby Bentleys that celebrated the coachbuilders' skills. It was no surprise to learn that the design team for the 2003 Continental GT turned for inspiration to the 1950s Continental.

However, some research into Bentley history by the designers of the 1991 Continental R – a model that was part of the belated resurrection of the name at the end of the century – also turned up another elegant but lesser-known

Bentley from a slightly earlier period. For John Heffernan and Ken Greenley, the independent designers commissioned by Rolls-Royce to create a modern Continental out of the Mulsanne Turbo saloon, the 1948 Bentley Cresta was like a preview to the famous Mulliner Continental of four years later.

The Cresta was conceived for Walter Sleator, a Rolls-Royce director and head of Franco-Britannic Autos, the firm's retailer in Paris, by the man who went on to found the short-lived Facel Vega car company. The idea was to use a Mk VI chassis to create a two-door Bentley grand tourer that would appeal to European buyers. The man Sleator selected to do the job was Jean Daninos, whose company Facel Metallon built 17 Bentley Crestas. One was the work of designer Pinin Farina (his company was later to become known as Pininfarina, and still is) in Turin and featured a wide, distinctly non-Bentley grille. Another was a clear indication of what Daninos's later Facel Vegas of 1954-64 would be like. But the majority carried elegant fastback bodywork more appropriate for a modern Bentley. Their headlights were mounted on the tops of the front wings, which carried straight through to the sloping rear rather than falling and rising around the rear wheels. The body-coloured grille surround carried a chromed insert and was reminiscent of the Humbers of the day.

Speed machine: The Continental R-type was the fastest four-seater in the world at the time of its introduction in 1952. Just over 200 were produced.

Fast fastback: When the longer S chassis replaced the R in 1955, Mulliner continued the memorable Continental coupe theme. Around another 430 were made.

Everyone at Rolls-Royce would have been familiar with the Crestas when work began in 1950 on the development of what was known at the time as the Corniche II. It was a reference to the ill-fated high-performance Bentley coupé that would (but for World War II) have been launched in 1940. For the post-war cars, the design team used the Mk VI chassis, which in 1952 gained a larger boot to become the R-type. The resulting Continental R-Type, unvelled in February 1952, was initially fitted with a high compression 4.6-litre version of the Mk VI's six-cylinder engine, later enlarged to 4.9 litres.

What everyone remembers about the Continental, though, is the lightweight coachwork built by H.J. Mulliner in Chiswick, London. The weight reduction was achieved by discarding the standard steel body of the R-Type saloon in favour of an aluminium alloy frame covered by aluminium body panels. The combination of the engine's higher power output, the sleek shape of the body (tested in Rolls-Royce's aero engine wind tunnel) and the weight reductions made the two-door Continental coupé the high performance car of the day. When the Continental achieved 120mph on the Montlhéry race track near Paris, it officially became the fastest four-seater in the world. The same target was set for Volkswagen's Bentley Continental GT half a century later.

The Continental R was not just fast, quiet and refined by the standards of the day. By most reckonings, it was, and remains, visually stunning. The shape of the car is often attributed to John Blatchley, the former Gurney Nutting stylist who went on to design Rolls-Royce's two major post-war successes, the Silver Cloud and Silver Shadow. The modest Blatchley will have none of it. 'My contribution might have been the original concept, but I never did any of the working drawings,' the 90-year-old Blatchley recalled in 2003. 'Evernden designed the car in conjunction with Mulliner.'

While Blatchley was Rolls-Royce's chief styling engineer at the time, Ivan Evernden was the company's chief project engineer. Stanley Watts was

Head-turner: The dashing
Continental coupe caught
the imagination of
car-starved Britons in the
1950s. It still does.

Variation of a theme: Not all Continental Rs featured Mulliner coachwork. The 1954 model on these pages was commissioned from Pinin Farina in Turin.

Mulliner's chief designer and the new model came from their team work. Blatchley added: 'Evernden gave me some credit for it (the Continental), but I don't feel it's right. I had some early input, but it's how you struggle with the realities, all the calculations, to make it work that counts.'

The Continental's beauty came at the daunting price of just over $19,000/£7,600, at a time when the standard R-type cost under $11,000/£4,400 and everyday cars could be had (subject to availability during a time of scarcity) for a few hundred pounds. That may explain why only 208 Continental Rs were built in the three years before the group replaced the whole range with the Silver Cloud and S-Type in 1955. All but a handful of them were built with the peerless Mulliner bodywork.

The unmistakable Bentley grille, proud and upright, featured the characteristic chrome surround and vertical slats. It was flanked by fared-in headlights and air vents, which blended artfully into the front wings. Each wing had a crease on the top and a descending swage line along the side. The rear wheels were encased in streamlined, elongated pods that were part of the body but appeared to be separate. Combined with the long bonnet, set-forward front wheels, sloping rear roofline and long rear overhang, everything spelled speed. The overall effect was that of the muscular athlete at the peak of fitness. Coming so soon after the country's uplifting Festival of Britain exhibition, the Continental R oozed confidence entirely appropriate to

Neo-Bentley? A post-war
Continental S3 and a pre-war
Derby saloon. Neither model
contained any of the
characteristics of the cars
designed by the company
founder.

Queen Elizabeth II's coronation year. It was the obvious form of transport for
James Bond, Ian Fleming's then newly created gentleman spy,

Where did its inspiration come from? The answer, according to one of the
few people who was around at the time, was from everyone else. Blatchley
recalled: 'When I was at Gurney Nutting, we used to visit every Paris motor
show. Then when I was at Rolls-Royce we went to Geneva and Turin as well.
I got all my ideas from motor shows like those. I'd look at something and
think, 'That's nice" and then try to adapt it.' He remembered being impressed
by some General Motors models of the late 1940s, but could not recall which
specific ones.

Half a century on, modern car designers would cheerfully acknowledge
little has changed since then. But it is one thing to purloin an idea, quite
another to turn it into an appropriate production feature on another make.
Blatchley's 1955 Silver Cloud, for example, is a fairly conventional design of
the day, but the secret of its enduring appeal is that the lines and proportions
were right. Today, the car still looks good from any angle. Blatchley's Silver
Shadow of 1965 went on to become the most popular Rolls-Royce of all time.

It is hard to believe, then, that someone as creative as John Blatchley
decided to walk away from Rolls-Royce at the height of his career. His time at
Gurney Nutting in the 1930s and at Rolls-Royce after the war meant that he
had probably designed more Bentleys (and other fine cars) than anyone else,
yet he retired in 1969 while still in his mid-50s. He did not give the company
or the motor industry a backward glance. 'At Rolls-Royce, I never had the
impression my work was appreciated at all,' he said shortly after a 90th
birthday party organised for him by the Rolls-Royce Enthusiasts Club.

Mulliner's great Continental look continued in slightly modified form
when the S replaced the R in 1955, but it was gone after the release of the
second Series S in 1959. That was the year Rolls-Royce bought Mulliner,

"The country's coach-building tradition all-but disappeared with the introduction of the modern, monocoque Silver Shadow and T series in 1965"

which was merged with its Park Ward coachbuilding company two years later. While the Continental name lived on in the second and third series of the S, it was frequently with less memorable bodies by Mulliner, Hooper, Young and Park Ward. In total, Continentals of various types accounted for around 15 per cent of the almost 7,500 Bentley S-Types made during its decade in production. The name and the country's coach-building tradition then all but disappeared with the introduction of the modern, monocoque Silver Shadow and T Series in 1965.

Those cars were very well received by buyers. Generally increasing wealth in Britain, where credit became easier to obtain, and in the rest of the world turned the range into the most popular Rolls-Royce of the modern era. The success put the car division in its strongest position for years, which was fortuitous because the parent company had by then become bogged down by appalling troubles in the aero engine business. Its impact on the car business was devastating.

Continental roots: When a young Brazilian designer called Raul Pires first saw a 1950s Continental at Crewe in the late 1990s, he quickly drew this sketch. It was the starting point for the 2003 Continental GT.

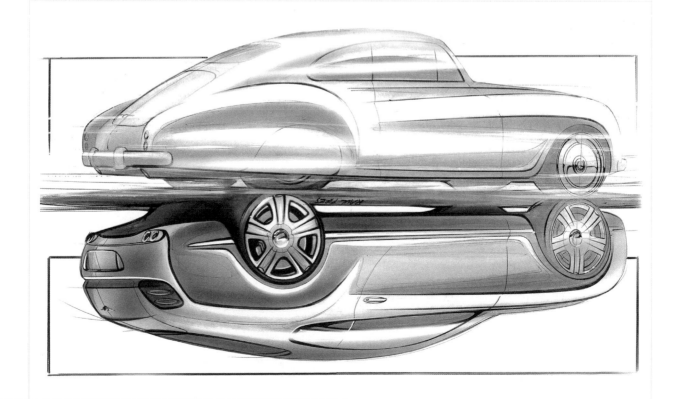

"When the parent company began to turn down requests for new equipment for the factory, it was their first inkling of the true scale of the RB-211 fiasco"

Chapter 8

Back from the brink

The bankruptcy of Rolls-Royce in February 1971 was a humbling episode for the company, and for Britain as a whole. Rolls-Royce was its industrial standard-bearer around the world, a symbol of engineering excellence that was a synonym for top quality. Rolls-Royce's problems revolved around a new type of aero engine known as RB-211. To win the contract to supply RB-211s for the new wide-body Douglas DC10, Rolls-Royce desperately made a series of promises it had no hope of meeting. Despite using new composites technology in an engine twice as powerful as anything it had previously made, Rolls-Royce agreed to impossible performance criteria, delivery dates and prices. It was several promises too far.

None of that had anything directly to do with the motor car division, where the relatively new Silver Shadow and T Series were selling very well. Such was their popularity that used cars were even changing hands for more money than new ones. However, executives at the car business became concerned towards the end of the 1960s when the parent company began to turn down requests for new equipment for the factory. It was their first inkling of the true scale of the RB-211 fiasco.

One of the first actions of the receiver, Rupert Nicholson, of Peat, Marwick & Mitchell, was to establish Rolls-Royce Motors Ltd as a separate, stand-alone business. It constituted barely 5 per cent of the group's sales turnover, but, as a profitable unit, it would clearly be saleable at some point in the future. David Plastow, the car division's former sales director, was appointed as its managing director one month before the group collapsed. It was his job to hold the car company together during that uncertain period.

Sign of the times: The Continental R was the first Bentley that did not have to share its shape with a Rolls-Royce in almost four decades.

Twenty-seven months later, in May 1973, Rolls-Royce Motors was listed on the London Stock Exchange. Its prospects looked good – except that five months after that, Syria and Egypt invaded Israel in what became known as the Yom Kippur War.

The effect on the world's economies was cataclysmic, as energy prices soared, consumption slowed and growth stopped. The imposition of an energy-saving 50mph speed limit in Britain found echoes around the world. It now seems astonishing that a tiny independent company whose sole products were 10 to 12 mpg limousines should have survived that period, especially as it was obliged to devote half its research and development budget to measures that would ensure it complied with growing safety and emissions regulations. Somehow, though, Rolls-Royce survived and once again showed its tenacity in the face of a fresh problem.

In at the deep end: David Plastow held the cars division together during the difficult period after the 1971 aerospace collapse.

Ancient and modern: When Rolls-Royce started to revive Bentley with the Turbo R, it used vintage Bentleys to provide a link with the past.

Under the circumstances, it is not surprising that Rolls-Royce paid scant attention to its Bentley brand. The company needed to concentrate its sales effort on the United States, the wealthiest and largest national market in the world. For that, it used its best card – Rolls-Royce. In comparison, Bentley at the time was the joker in terms of US public awareness. Perhaps the real achievement is that Bentley in the mid-1970s did not suffer the fate of some other famous marques. Jensen went out of business, Citroen abandoned its Maserati company, Ferruccio Lamborghini sold his interest in the car company he had only recently created, and David Brown finally gave up an unequal struggle at Aston Martin Lagonda.

Demand for Rolls-Royces picked up as the decade progressed when economies gradually came out of their troughs. The company was sufficiently confident in 1977 to commit funds to the development of a new generation of cars. They were needed, because the Silver Shadow and T Series were by then 12 years old. The following year, the company's annual sales hit an unprecedented level of more than 3,300, though in the UK the decade drew to a close under the shadow of a protracted miners' strike and three-day working week. In 1979, the Shah of Iran was deposed, and energy prices soared once again.

It became increasingly clear to Rolls-Royce management that it was too small, too vulnerable, to remain as an independent company. Even the giant companies of the motor industry were suffering, so how could tiny Rolls-Royce prosper? The results of that thinking became clear in June 1980, when Rolls-Royce merged with the larger Vickers industrial group. In a clever reference to Vickers' role as one of the country's leading defence contractors, the two came together following a series of discussions code-named War and

Comeback kid: The 1991
Continental R coupe helped
with the Bentley revival began
a few years earlier.

Peace. In reality, it was more of a Vickers takeover. Then, in September, the new Rolls-Royce Silver Spirit and Bentley Mulsanne were released. It really was the start of a new era for the two brands.

The two new models were clearly derived from their 15-year-old predecessors. Engines, transmissions and chassis components were carried over, but they were given new three-box bodywork designed by Fritz Feller, Rolls-Royce's renaissance man – an engineer who was to become head of design. There was very little apart from the grilles and badges to distinguish one from the other, but there was one encouraging sign that Bentley's heritage had at last been remembered. Mulsanne is the name of the straight on the Le Mans race circuit where the Bentley legend was forged in the 1920s. It was a start. Two years later, there was another positive signal, when a higher-performance turbocharged version of the Mulsanne went into the catalogue. The Turbo initially proved a coarse and unreliable machine, but the subsequent Turbo R when fitted with fuel injection went a long way towards re-establishing the credibility of Bentley.

" They began the process by which Bentley once more came to out-sell Rolls-Royce "

Whatever was said at the time, though, the Turbo was not an example of Bentley going back to its roots: neither is the turbocharging on the 2003 models. The method of forced induction has varied – by exhaust pressure on the modern cars, by mechanical means on the vintage cars – but the whole concept was alien to the engineering ideals of W.O. Bentley. At the end of the 1920s, he had fought Tim Birkin's idea of supercharging and never changed his view.

With Vickers responsibilities to attend to after the merger, Plastow was replaced at Rolls-Royce by George Fenn. The first half of the 1980s then became a period of revolving doors at Crewe. Fenn retired, and was followed shortly afterwards by his replacement, Dick Perry. In the meanwhile, Vickers began to recruit some younger outsiders who were destined to shake up Crewe's cloistered existence. Two of the key newcomers joined Rolls Royce on the same day in February 1983.

Mike Dunn, a former top engineer at Alvis, Leyland and Ford, became Rolls-Royce's engineering director. His job was to introduce big-company disciplines to Rolls-Royce's engineering department, which was a law to itself. It was more powerful than the company's sales and marketing department, which, in the absence of product planners, effectively meant engineering dictated the type of car Rolls-Royce made. Until 1985, Rolls-Royce made its own nuts and bolts, for example, when they could have been bought for a fraction of the cost from a specialist supplier. True to its traditions, Crewe built soft, floaty cars with a premium on ride, refinement and silence, just as it always had. But, seemingly unnoticed in Crewe, consumer tastes had changed. Wealthy, younger customers wanted faster, sharper cars with better cornering ability. They wanted BMWs and Mercedes-Benz, Porsches and Jaguars. Dunn's job was to take Rolls-Royce and Bentley forward without alienating existing customers.

Peter Ward's was the other critical appointment at the time. Ward had been working in the component sector (mainly Unipart and Motaquip) before becoming Rolls-Royce marketing director in 1973. When Perry left, Ward was appointed managing director in late 1986 and chief executive six months later. In that position, he was able to do something about an aspect of Rolls-Royce's car history that had been dormant for too long. It was time for a proper Bentley revival. The actions taken by Ward and his colleagues from the middle of 1980s had the effect of transforming the shape of the Rolls-Royce car business. They began the process by which Bentley once more came to outsell Rolls-Royce.

If the 1982 Mulsanne Turbo marked the end of Bentley neglect, it did so in a slightly curious way. Since W.O. Bentley's first cars, Bentley grilles had

The cars that never were: The Bentley P90 concept coupe (left) was unveiled in 1985, but designers Heffernan and Greenley secretly developed a parallel Rolls-Royce as a potential Corniche convertible replacement. Neither car made it to production.

been finished in shiny chrome metal, but the practice was abandoned with the Turbo. Its grilles were body-coloured and the effect was more in keeping with the moment – more subtle, less brazen – and it was not long before the look was adopted for all Bentleys. The designers of the Continental GT two decades later had no hesitation in specifying coloured grilles, even if chrome plate was the way W.O. would have wanted to see them.

The Bentley revival accelerated with the Eight of 1984 and the following year's R version of the Turbo. The Eight, which was a slightly cheaper version of the Mulsanne, retained the traditional chrome grille surround, and accompanied it with chromed wire mesh that picked up the design theme of the first Bentleys. The car was conceived to appeal to buyers of top-model Mercedes-Benz and BMWs, though the project carried an element of risk by taking the Bentley brand a degree downmarket. The Turbo R represented an engineering upgrade of the Turbo with many of the flaws taken out and, thanks to Dunn, considerably improved road-holding and handling. When the model was equipped with Bosch fuel injection two years later, its performance became truly world class.

Rolls-Royce had even higher ambitions for Bentley around that time. The company asked for a Bentley concept coupé from a couple of the UK motor industry's most talented independent designers, John Heffernan and Ken Greenley. The Royal College of Art lecturers had already designed the

Modern Bentley Boy: Peter Ward instigated the Bentley revival when he became head of Rolls-Royce Motor Cars in the mid-1980s.

Overleaf: Quick change: It is not generally know that the origins of the Continental R coupe concept (right) stem from a plan to develop a Rolls-Royce Corniche convertible replacement (left). Heffernan and Greenley created the Bentley from their earlier work on the Rolls-Royce.

Panther Solo sports car – a project that never went into production because Toyota launched the MR2 – and were secretly working on a concept that was unveiled at the 1985 Geneva motor show as Project 90.

It was commissioned by Rolls-Royce's first product planning director, John Stephenson, another of the new generation of outsiders who joined the company in 1993. The car, which was known internally as the Black Rat because of its colour, was a mock-up fabricated by International Automotive Design, but it looked the part. IAD was a contract engineering consultancy working for most of the world's major car companies at various times (it is no longer in business).

It was therefore a surprise when, a few weeks later, the company quashed outside expectations that it would be turned into a production reality. A number of reasons have been put forward. First, the Rolls-Royce board felt the design was too much like the Lincoln Continental and would date very quickly. The company also had to address manufacturing inefficiencies at Crewe before it could embark on any new project. But perhaps most telling of all, a production version of the Bentley P90 would have cost more to build than the Mulsanne limousine, yet was expected to carry a lower price. Whatever the truth, John Stephenson abruptly resigned when his pet project was cancelled.

What is not widely known is that Heffernan and Greenley, together with IAD, simultaneously used the P90 to produce another glassfibre concept car – for a Rolls-Royce Corniche convertible replacement. A new Corniche was overdue because it had been around since 1971, but Rolls-Royce decided its priority was to address its internal production problems. The Corniche was canned, just like the P90, though the idea did not go away. Heffernan and Greenley struck off in another direction for the Corniche replacement, but the result of their work was not revealed until 1991. When it was, it was with a coupé that faithfully resurrected the spirit of the 1950s Bentley Continental R.

All in all, then, the late 1980s were great for the brand the world almost forgot. It was the decade when Bentley was reborn. Rolls-Royce began to use the term 'Bentley Motors' once more, a clear indication of the marque's growing importance. The sales returns tell the story. By the time the Silver Shadow and T series were replaced in 1980, Bentley versions accounted for fewer than 5 per cent of the group's sales. At the time, there were even Rolls-Royce labels on the engine rocker covers and instruments of the few Bentley versions. But the product expansion on the basis of the Mulsanne manifestly touched a chord with car buyers. By 1990, Bentleys constituted 52 per cent of group sales, which that year reached a record of over 3,300. It was the first time since the immediate post-war period that Bentley achieved more

"The late 1980s were great for the brand the world almost forgot. It was the decade when Bentley was re-born"

significant numbers than Rolls-Royce. The process became even more pronounced as the following decade unfolded.

The model that Heffernan and Greenley laboured over in the late 1980s and early 1990s was the landmark Continental R that was unveiled to great acclaim at the 1991 Geneva motor show. It was Rolls-Royce's first dedicated Bentley since the Continental R-Type almost four decades earlier. However, the athletic two-door coupé, which was based on the mechanical components of the Turbo R, began development as a proposal known as CXA to replace the ageing Corniche. The project took on a new dynamic after Ward replaced Perry as managing director. Ward and his colleagues presented the designers with the task of transforming the CXA, which was completed with all the design language of a Rolls-Royce, into something that clearly looked like a Bentley. What was more, they had to do so without altering the car's fixed engineering features, or hard points as they are known in the motor industry. 'It wasn't a simple task,' Heffernan recalled in 2003.

While the Rolls-Royce CXA was restrained and conservative, with almost geometric straight lines, the Bentley CXA was more sporty and sophisticated, with curvy shapes that created pools of light. The concept's early Greco-

Breath of fresh air: The Azure convertible appeared in 1995, four years after the Continental R on which it was based. The car was made in conjunction with Pininfarina.

Where's the money?
Heffernan and Greenley were
not short of ideas for Bentley's
future design direction, such
as this concept coupe from
the early 1990s. All that was
missing was the money to pay
for them.

Roman Rolls-Royce grille was replaced by a Bentley nose job, albeit body-coloured, and the headlights were changed from oblong units to four round lights. At the rear, the lights were given a more upright look. At the same time, the boot lid height was increased for better high-speed stability. The task was to create an integrated boot lid spoiler without making it look like one. It was a relatively new design trick at the time, but one that is now quite often used by designers.

The reborn Continental R comfortably outperformed all Rolls-Royce sales expectations for it, in spite of an audacious price tag in the region of $289,000/£170,000. The subsequent convertible version known as the Azure was even more expensive at around $365,000/£215,000. But when the engineering work for the Azure roof mechanism was assigned to Pininfarina, Heffernan and Greenley felt slighted. 'It was what we did in the first place, but we didn't know the car existed until it was announced,' Greenley later said.

There is no doubt about the range's commercial success, however. The Continental and Azure proved to be high earners at a difficult time for the company, which put the project's development cost at only $32 million£19 million. The Continental's debut at the 1991 Geneva show also provided arguably the most astonishing piece of luck enjoyed by Rolls-Royce.

Driver's eye view: The interiors of the Continental and Azure were sumptuously hand finished with a profusion of wood veneers and leather.

The early 1990s saw demand for cars around the world drop dramatically. Rolls-Royce and Bentley were not alone, but the company had to endure a sudden plunge from the record 3,300-plus sales of 1990 to around 1,400 in each of the three years 1992-94. Things improved a bit after that, but not by much. Yet that was the time when Rolls-Royce had to make a major investment in order to bring out a new generation of cars in 1998. In other words, it had a considerably lower income at a time when it needed more. Yet Rolls-Royce reported return on sales ratios that were among the best in the business at the time. They were as high as 10 per cent for a sector that considers 5 per cent to be an achievement. And what was good for Rolls-Royce was good for its parent, Vickers.

How did Rolls-Royce do it? The answer lay in the Sultanate of Brunei, a tiny country in south-east Asia that is stupendously wealthy thanks to seemingly endless deposits of oil and natural gas. Prince Jefri, the country's finance minister, adores fast cars, the more expensive and rarer the better. The Continental R that appeared in Geneva that March was one of the catalysts that led the prince, together with his oldest son, Prince Hakeem, to start a private collection of the best cars in the world.

> **"** The re-born Continental R comfortably out-performed all Rolls-Royce sales expectations for it, in spite of an audacious price tag **"**

Growing apart: The Mulsanne series, launched in parallel with the Rolls-Royce Silver Spirit, was the foundation of the Bentley revival and led to the Eight and Turbo R.

The collection was put together in utmost secrecy, but Bentleys were known to be particular favourites. Of more than 3,500 vehicles of all types that were believed to have been bought by Prince Jefri and Prince Hakeem by the end of the decade, over 650 were made in Crewe. That is disproportionately high for a company the size of Rolls-Royce. Some of the orders were for Rolls-Royces, but they were mostly for Bentleys. Many were very special Bentleys indeed. The orders became so numerous and varied that the Mulliner-Park Ward coachbuilding subsidiary of Rolls-Royce had to create a dedicated department to design, engineer and validate them. It was known as the Blackpool team, though the link with England's northern coastal resort is not clear.

The Bentleys included numerous four-door saloon and estate car versions of the two-door Continental R coupe, others with Range Rover four-wheel-drive transmissions and production versions of the Java concept car. Among the names they carried were Dominator, Buccaneer, Imperial, Phoenix, Spectre, Pegasus, Rapier, Val d'Isere, Silverstone and Camelot. Sadly, none of them has been seen in public, and are unlikely to be. Most are kept in air-conditioned warehouses in Brunei, where they are guarded by soldiers of the Gurkha Regiment.

Overtaking manouevre: The Continental R helped to push Bentley sales past those of Rolls-Royce during the final decade of the 20th century.

While the Brunei purchases are not directly germane to the Bentley story, they were extremely profitable to Rolls-Royce. They had the effect of underwriting the Rolls-Royce business plan during the mid-1990s, which revolved around the design and development of the new Silver Seraph and Arnage for 1998. The orders therefore also indirectly supported Vickers, the London-listed public company that was a major defence contractor to the UK government.

All good things must end. Prince Jefri's high spending with Rolls-Royce – and with AMG, Aston Martin, Ferrari, Mercedes-Benz, Pininfarina, Porsche and other purveyors of the world's finest cars – dried up towards the end of the 1990s, when the economies of Asia succumbed to economic meltdown. They began to recover a few years later, but Jefri had not returned to big-time car buying by the end of 2003. The world's top car makers live in hope that he will, of course.

It was against that background that the importance of Bentley within Rolls-Royce continued to grow. The proportion of Bentleys sold by the company each year went up to 61 per cent in 1995 and to 73 per cent when the new millennium began. That was wonderful for Bentley, but what the trend also indicated was that demand for Rolls-Royces began heading for oblivion. What an irony: one reason Rolls-Royce Motor Cars survived the last two decades of the 20th century was that it revived the brand it had spent the previous two decades ignoring. It was a *de facto* reversal of Rolls-Royce's 1931 takeover of Bentley.

"It was a de *facto reversal* of Rolls-Royce's 1931 take-over of Bentley"

"Vickers...made discrete inquiries among some of the world's biggest car groups about whether they would like to buy its famous brands"

Chapter 9

All change

For sale: A few months before the Bentley Arnage was due to be launched, Vickers shocked the world with its decision to sell Rolls-Royce and Bentley.

The end of the 20th century brought no more stability to the Rolls-Royce and Bentley brands than all the previous years of turbulence. The 1990s were both decisive and divisive for their future. When the decade began, the two were more or less equal partners in terms of worldwide sales, though one was on the up and the other on its way down. By the time it ended, they were competitors for the first time since the start of the 1930s. Both, though, were obliged to forfeit true control of their own destinies in the process.

The big car issue for Vickers in the early 1990s was how to replace the Silver Spirit and Mulsanne series that had been on sale since 1980. They were already very old by car industry standards, especially as much of their technology was a legacy of the previous Silver Shadow and T Series that was originally introduced in 1965. Internally, Rolls-Royce knew what would be required to modernise its cars, but the challenge was to do so on a limited budget. The parent group propped up the car company to the tune of around $1.7 million/£1 million a week during the recession in the early part of the decade. It was a bad experience for Vickers and its shareholders, who were in no mood to throw yet more money at its unpredictable car business.

Indeed, Vickers was so disturbed by the poor sales performance of Rolls-Royce Motor Cars during 1991-92 that it made discrete inquiries among some of the world's biggest car groups about whether they would like to buy its famous brands. There was a lot of polite interest, but none of the potential purchasers understood the mega-money limousine market. Curiously, in view of what happened a few years later, there were no takers. With no buyers for the company and the pressing matter of the new generation cars, Vickers had no option but to carry on. Its compromise solution was unprecedented, and went to the heart of whether Vickers really understood the nature of the car business and the heritage of the nameplates it controlled.

Historically, Rolls-Royce (and Bentley until it was taken over) always made its own engines and used bodywork supplied by outside contractors, initially a variety of small coachbuilders and in more recent times by the Pressed Steel company. The controversial proposal was to reverse tradition by making the bodyshells internally at Crewe and buying engines from an outside supplier. At an estimated $255 million/£150 million, bringing the new cars to market was an expensive undertaking by the company's standards, though a high-volume car group would almost regard the sum as loose change. Still, it would be much cheaper for Rolls-Royce and Bentley than developing new bodies and new engines.

To the surprise of outsiders, the engine supplier would not be Cosworth Engineering, the specialist drivetrain company bought by Vickers as recently as 1990. Cosworth's origins were in motor sport, but by that time it had built a substantial business in engine development and assembly and as a light alloy castings supplier to the mainstream motor industry.

Cosworth sold road car engine expertise to General Motors, Ford and Mercedes-Benz, the groups its sister company, Rolls-Royce, turned to when it began looking for the engines it would need for its 1998 models. The development raised the question of what the rationale was behind Vickers' purchase of Cosworth.

In the end, the big engine supply decision came down to a straight contest between Mercedes-Benz and BMW. It was a choice overlaid by latent emotion in Britain because of memories of the 1939-45 conflict against Germany, and the military roles played by each of the companies in their respective countries. From the perspective of the modern international motor industry, though, there were no other options. Each of the giant German groups offered to sell V12s for the forthcoming Rolls-Royce and turbocharged V8s for the Bentley version. When Rolls-Royce evaluated each engine in each proposed chassis, it came to the conclusion that the Mercedes option was preferable. If only the decision had been that simple. Vickers was lobbied hard from the opposite direction by BMW and its partner in an aero engine joint venture, Rolls-Royce plc, which was by then a separate company. Political expedient triumphed over engineering solution. When the board of Vickers elected at the end of 1994 to take the BMW route, Peter Ward, the Rolls-Royce Motor Cars chief executive who endorsed the Mercedes offer, felt obliged to resign. He was replaced by Chris Woodwark, who had recently joined the group to run Cosworth.

New broom: The Crewe factory that had turned out Bentleys and Rolls-Royces for the previous half-century was the beneficiary of unprecedented investment after the ownership change.

With the engine contract agreed, Rolls-Royce Motor Cars had four years to design, develop and certify the two models the world came to know as the Bentley Arnage and Rolls-Royce Silver Seraph. The engineer put in charge of the project was Tony Gott, a man who was later to play significant roles at both Bentley and Rolls-Royce after they were sold by Vickers. For Bentley, the positive news was that, for the first time since the early days under Rolls-Royce ownership, its engines would be different from those of Rolls-Royce. It was one more step towards the eventual separation of the two stablemates that had once been rivals.

In the meanwhile, though, they had to share the same four-door body-chassis unit, which was developed with the aid of the Mayflower engineering consultancy and was destined to be assembled in a section of the Crewe factory that produced the company's long-running 6.75-litre V8 engines. Within that limitation, Rolls-Royce designers and engineers did what they could to differentiate the two products. The difficulty was that they had a bronze budget to achieve a gold standard. While the Rolls-Royce (known internally as P2000) was to be limousine-like, soft and silent, the Bentley (P3000) had to have a more overt sporty look and feel. The company decided that the words that best characterised Bentley were 'certainty, passion, daring, stamina and thoroughbred'. In other words, a Bentley should have attitude, just as it had in the 1920s.

The Rolls-Royce got softer seats and tyres, a purring exhaust note and a column-mounted gear shift lever, but everything in the Bentley was firmer, including the suspension, tyres and the more wraparound seats. The car had a centre console and a centrally mounted lever with sportier change-up points for the automatic. The large-bore exhausts were very visible and tuned to produce a distinct rumble. The egg box-style grille in brushed welded stainless steel was distinctly aggressive. Unlike the Rolls-Royce, the Bentley had a prominent rev counter, which was complemented by other parchment-coloured instruments and more adventurous treatments for the interior, including the use of wood.

It's a deal: Sir Ralph Robins (left) of Rolls-Royce plc, Bernd Pischetsrieder of BMW (centre) and Ferdinand Piech of Volkswagen celebrate the deal that split Rolls-Royce and Bentley.

Under the circumstances, the company did a good job at reviving the look and sound of the Bentley spirit. Visually, it was a good interpretation of what W.O. Bentley might have done to create a late 20th-century saloon. But there was one significant problem. The engine selected for the Bentley was BMW's light alloy V8 displacing 4.4 litres. What it had in common with W.O.'s own four- and six-cylinder engines were four valves per cylinder, though the German unit used four overhead camshafts to operate them rather than W.O.'s single overhead camshaft. Rolls-Royce's internal reservations centred on the BMW engine's refinement, weight and power output. Would it be good enough to produce the high performance associated with a Bentley?

For example, installed in the BMW 7-Series, a car that weighed nearly 4,100 pounds, the engine produced 286 horsepower and 310 pounds/feet of torque at 3,900 rpm. But the Arnage was to have a much larger frontal area and was destined to tip the scales at virtually 1,000 pounds more than the 7-Series. Unless the engine could be tuned to give a lot more power and torque, the performance of the Arnage would be anaemic.

The task of doing something about the engine was handed to Cosworth, which fitted twin Garrett turbochargers and made other appropriate modifications to boost the V8's output to 354 horsepower and its torque to 420 pounds/feet at 2,500 rpm. In other words, the Arnage had 24 per cent more power and 36 per cent more torque than the 7-Series. However, it was barely enough to overcome the 24 per cent weight penalty the Bentley had over the BMW.

Eager Bentley enthusiasts were able to do the mathematics once the car was released in the spring of 1998. They were not greatly impressed, as early sales indicated. Neither was the new owner of the Bentley brand when it took over a few months later. Volkswagen's No. 1 priority was to turn the Arnage into the really high performance saloon it should have been in the first place.

Earlier evidence that Bentley was in the ascendant at Crewe came in a 1994 concept car known as Java or MSB (medium size Bentley). The

> **"** Volkswagen's No.1 priority was to turn the Arnage into the really high performance saloon it should have been in the first place **"**

company's vision was to offer a cheaper range of Bentleys – four-door saloon, two-door coupe and convertible – at prices ranging from $112,500/£75,000 to $150,000/£100,000. That would have put the brand more directly in competition with the top-line BMW or Mercedes-Benz models that were proving so popular with new City money and young entrepreneurs.

Java, which was based on the platform of the BMW 5-Series, was fully engineered and costed by a team of Bentley and BMW engineers working in Munich. However, it never got beyond the project stage because the British company was fully occupied by the development of the P2000 and P3000. It had neither the manpower nor the money to produce a third model simultaneously. There were also internal reservations about whether the project contained too much BMW and not enough Bentley. However, the fact that Volkswagen subsequently came to broadly similar conclusions concerning an MSB-type vehicle was an endorsement of the mid-1990s concept. The Java project was never formally presented to the Vickers board for approval, but it was still simmering when Rolls-Royce Motor Cars was overtaken by the dramatic events that started in October 1997.

Vickers decided it had had enough of Rolls-Royce ownership. The development was a shock to everyone, not least to Rolls-Royce Motor Cars chief executive Graham Morris, who was on holiday at the time. Morris had been persuaded to leave Audi six months earlier to take the Rolls-Royce job when Woodwark became chief operating officer of Vickers. Morris did so on the understanding that Rolls-Royce would not be sold, but he was misled.

What the world did not know when the sale notices went up at Rolls-Royce was that it was the start of the gradual break-up of Vickers itself, an industrial group whose history went back to the 19th century. Vickers shareholders did nicely out of the process.

The final couple of months of 1997 and the first half of the following year were tremendously stressful for everyone who worked for Rolls-Royce/Bentley and Vickers. Internally, the main concern was to make sure the launches of the new products took place on schedule, the Silver Seraph at the Geneva motor show in March and the Arnage at the Le Mans race track the following month. It was not as if the company was well practised in these things, because new car introductions were rarities at Crewe. Nevertheless, they went ahead on time and on budget.

The big drama was played out far from Crewe at Vickers' headquarters in London and in various car capitals of the world. Suddenly, there was a lot of interest in Rolls-Royce and Bentley, from well-intentioned amateur enthusiasts to venture capitalists and some of the top names in the global car business. Vickers wanted to hear only from people with serious money.

BMW, which then owned the Rover Group, was quick to declare an interest and was seen as the clear favourite because of its engine supply contract and some surreptitious technology-sharing with Rolls-Royce. What proved equally decisive, though, was something that was not fully understood by most people at the time, including the decision-makers at Vickers. While Rolls-Royce plc, the aero engine company, no longer had any formal business connections with the Rolls-Royce car maker, the former held the legal title to the use of the name and interlocked double-R badge. It freely granted the use to Vickers, but could veto its use by any company it did not approve. And with BMW and Rolls-Royce plc embarked on an aero engine joint venture, the German firm made sure its partners at the British aero engine company would support its takeover ambitions for the Rolls-Royce (and Bentley) car business. The connection proved critical.

Daimler-Benz, the owner of Mercedes-Benz, was more interested than it was prepared to admit, but abruptly withdrew from the contest in order to concentrate on another major deal. That, it later turned out, was the merger with Chrysler Corporation. Besides, Mercedes had already embarked on the Maybach project that would challenge Rolls-Royce and Bentley dominance of the limousine market early in the 21st century. Mercedes did not need Rolls-Royce or Bentley.

The real surprise was the Volkswagen group's declaration as a contender for Rolls-Royce and Bentley. Under Ferdinand Piëch, its ambitious chairman, Volkswagen had to be taken very seriously. Piëch was the one person who could derail what looked increasingly like a BMW shoo-in, and he did. Vickers shareholders initially voted for BMW's $545 million/£340 million offer and promised to invest $1.6 billion/£1 billion in Rolls-Royce and Bentley, only to change their minds shortly afterwards when Volkswagen offered an additional $145 million/£90 million and an investment commitment of $2.4 billion/£1.5 billion. As it was BMW policy from the start not to get involved in a bidding war, it looked as though Volkswagen had won. In order to make sure Vickers shareholders were paying proper attention, Volkswagen then agreed to buy Cosworth Engineering if its offer for the car brands was approved. The prospect of a cash windfall of nearly $960 million/£600 million (about $750 million/£470 million for Bentley, and around $190 million/£120 million for Cosworth) was simply too attractive to ignore. At an extraordinary general meeting in early June, Vickers shareholders approved the sale of Rolls-Royce, Bentley and Cosworth to the Volkswagen group.

The great Rolls-Royce and Bentley carve-up seemed to be all over, but it wasn't. Even before Vickers shareholders voted in favour of Volkswagen,

Bernd Pischetsrieder, the BMW chairman, and Sir Ralph Robins, the chairman of Rolls-Royce plc, made an outline agreement that, whatever happened, BMW would be granted the rights to use the Rolls-Royce name and emblem on cars for $64 million/£40 million. While the world was under the impression that Volkswagen was the new owner of the two famous British firms, Pischetsrieder and Piëch then secretly negotiated the compromise that resulted in BMW granting Volkswagen the rights to the Rolls-Royce name until the end of 2002, after which BMW formally took charge. In exchange, BMW acquired all the historic Rolls-Royce car names and the Spirit of Ecstasy statue, which were technically part of the sale to Volkswagen.

None of that became public knowledge until the end of July – some seven weeks later – when Pischetsrieder, Piëch and Robins confirmed the details of the final settlement at a packed press conference in London. All declared themselves pleased with the outcome. BMW got Rolls-Royce and immediately began preparing for the January 2003 transfer. Volkswagen got the Bentley brand, the Crewe factory and workforce, and the global distribution system.

Piëch was widely seen at the time as having been outsmarted by Pischetsrieder. We now know that was not the case. Piëch knew exactly what was going on thanks to the series of regular top-secret meetings he held with the BMW chairman over the previous weeks and months. Between them, they stitched together a mutually satisfactory division of the British motor industry's crown jewels. The two really were satisfied with their spending spree in Britain.

Piëch, who had seemed so uncomfortable at the July press conference, was quietly content. He had only ever wanted the Bentley brand because of its potential for much higher sales than Rolls-Royce.

The new man in charge of Bentley's destiny was a grandson of the founder of the Porsche engineering consultancy. At a time when W.O. Bentley was getting his fledgling car company off the ground in London, Ferdinand Porsche was technical director of Daimler in Stuttgart. Porsche subsequently went on to create his own sports car company, which employed his young grandson as technical director in the 1960s. Like W.O., Piëch loved motor racing and Le Mans, where his mighty Porsche 917s made such a major impact at the start of the 1970s. Given the histories of Bentley and the man who had just bought it, a Bentley return to Le Mans suddenly seemed less fanciful.

"The business reality was that the Volkswagen purchase was arguably the most positive development in the 79-year history of Bentley"

Chapter 10

A fresh start

The history of Bentley (and Rolls-Royce) was never dull. It involved a company failure, a financial rescue plan, a takeover, another company failure, moves to three different manufacturing centres, virtual oblivion, a merger and eventual regeneration. All that took place against a roller-coaster background of mighty sales peaks and troughs, world war, technological revolution, industry consolidation and globalisation. Then, in the middle of 1998, Bentley got another new owner, and ownership of another British company was moving overseas. On top of that, the owner was a global group based in Germany, the UK's enemy in two 20th century world wars, and a country many in Britain continued to regard coolly. The business reality though was that the Volkswagen acquisition was arguably the most positive development in the 79-year history of Bentley.

Volkswagen was created by Germany's National Socialist party in the 1930s to bring motorisation to the country's masses. That is what it eventually did, but not until Nazi ideas were no more than bad memories. From the post-war ruins of the town and the factory created in Wolfsburg, Lower Saxony, to produce the Beetle, Volkswagen steadily grew to become the largest automotive group in Europe and the fourth largest in the world. Under Ferdinand Piëch, the chairman, the group doubled in size during the 1990s. Volkswagen really understands the international car business.

Along the way, Volkswagen picked up ownership of Audi (the remains of the group that made the awesome Auto Union racing cars in the 1930s), Seat in Spain, Skoda in the Czech Republic and Lamborghini and Bugatti in Italy. That made the group more than just a manufacturer. Being responsible for

Back on track: Bentley returned to its happy hunting ground at Le Mans. The day after the 2003 event, the winning car was paraded along the Champs Elysée in Paris.

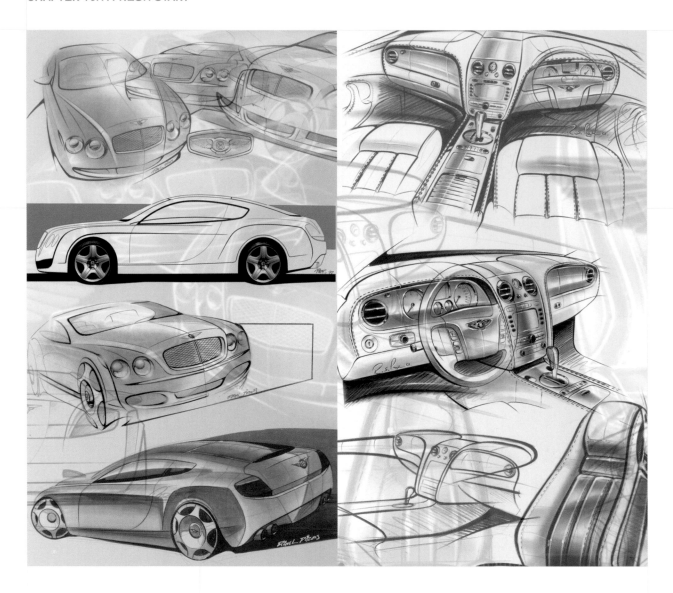

Way ahead: Under Volkswagen, Bentley assembled an international design team to create the new generation cars. These are some evolutionary sketches that resulted in the Continental GT.

companies that made different cars for different customers, Volkswagen had to learn the importance of branding and marketing. It was not initially that successful in this respect, but by the time of the Bentley purchase Volkswagen knew intuitively what would be right for the marque and its cherished DNA.

It meant starting afresh, because the only real value in Bentley was its name, and the craft skills of its woodworkers, leather stitchers and engine assemblers in Crewe. In terms of product, technology and sales revenue, the marque was an outdated anachronism. That it did not die of neglect was thanks only to a handful of Rolls-Royce visionaries, who pulled Bentley back from its near-death experience in the final two decades of the last century. Bentley's growing importance within the group during that time saw sales comprehensively eclipse those of Rolls-Royce. Everything Bentley achieved was on a shoestring budget, however. Volkswagen ownership meant that Bentley faced the future with proper funding. The folks at Crewe had never experienced anything like it.

But when Volkswagen promised to invest $850 million/£500 million in Bentley Motors over the following five years, the money was not

Family affair: In early 2004, Bentley made some gentle styling modifications to give the Arnage more of a Continental GT look. The twin round headlights are a give-away.

unconditional. The company and its employees had to perform, to shed archaic working practices and to agree to more flexible shift patterns. In short, Bentley had to cease being a cloistered and insular producer of rare automotive jewels and to become instead a full member of one of the world's major industrial groups. The staff members who began to drive daily to the factory in Crewe did so in leased Volkswagens, not clapped out Fords and Nissans. And they no longer worked at "Royce's" but at Bentley. The symbolism of the name change helped to make the transition. It was all worthwhile, because the prospects for Bentley and its factory had never been better.

The person most disturbed by the events of late 1997/early 1998 was Graham Morris, the chief executive of Rolls-Royce and Bentley. He felt betrayed that Vickers had not warned him of the sale decision. Then, in an attempt to restore morale at Crewe, Morris assured employees that the two brands would not be separated. When they were, he decided he could no longer remain as chief executive. Tony Gott, the engineering director, took over Morris's role when he resigned. The changes were part of a sweeping management restructuring shortly after the Volkswagen takeover. Bentley got new people responsible for sales and marketing, finance, engineering, manufacturing and design. It was all part of a new order and a new direction for Bentley.

The long-term strategy was to design and develop an all-new range of cars that would go into production in 2003. In the meanwhile, Volkswagen decided it needed to do something about the inadequate BMW-powered Arnage. Known as the Green Label, the model lasted in production only 18 months before being replaced in autumn 1999 by the Red Label. After an intensive engineering programme, a turbocharged version of the

"Bentley had to cease being a cloistered and insular producer of rare automotive jewels and to become instead a full member of one of the world's major industrial groups"

Money no object: Bentley reported in 2004 that over half of Arnage customers have their cars further personalised by its Mulliner coach-building subsidiary.

Rolls-Royce/Bentley's traditional 6.75-litre V8 was installed in the Arnage. The engine, which had been confined to history with the arrival of the first Arnage, was extensively reworked in order to comply with emissions regulations. The important aspect for customers, though, was that the Red Label boasted 405 horsepower (14 per cent more than the Green Label) and a massive 612 pounds/feet at 2,150 rpm, a torque increase of 46 per cent. The Arnage T of just over two years later then saw power rise to 457 horsepower and torque go up to 645 pounds/feet. In other words, the T had 62 per cent more power and more than double the torque of the 1998 model from which it was derived. It was enough to turn the Arnage into an appropriately high-performance model that properly reflected the Bentley heritage.

That heritage was drawn on when Bentley embarked on two other very high-profile projects that could not be more different: the return to the

The car's the star: After Bentley won at Le Mans in 2003, a celebration dinner at London's Savoy Hotel echoed the same event after its 1927 victory.

Déjà-vu: Getting the winning 1927 Le Mans-winning Bentley into the Savoy Hotel was a logistical challenge (above). It was no easier in 2003 (opposite page).

Le Mans race track and the creation of a new state limousine for Queen Elizabeth II. One reached back to the company's roots, but the other was a fresh opportunity for Bentley because Britain's royal family traditionally favoured Rolls-Royces and, before that, Daimlers as state vehicles. Simultaneously extending the Bentley brand as pure racing cars and as a royal carriage for the first time represented a brand challenge. However, both developments were wonderful morale boosts for the firm that had so recently nearly died. They added to the newly found confidence at Crewe. On this occasion, Bentley had the resources and the finances to enable the jobs to be completed to the highest standard.

But top line motor racing had been transformed since W.O.'s days. Modern racing cars cannot double as road cars, as they once could, so Bentley had to enlist the expertise of some racing specialists. It commissioned the design and development of its sports-racers from a British company, Racing Technology Norfolk (the outfit responsible for the highly successful Audi R8 racers), and assigned the team management to Apex Motorsport. Team Bentley's EXP Speed 8s also borrowed the 3.6-litre twin-turbo V8 developed for Audi, its sister company within the Volkswagen group.

Time was in short supply. The programme was announced only at the end of 2000, but the intention was to compete at Le Mans in three successive

years, starting seven months later. Team Bentley estimated – correctly as it turned out – that it would require three years for any new team to achieve victory. It got off to an excellent start with a third place to the all-conquering Audis in the rain-soaked 2001 event. The following year, with a modified car and a 4-litre direct injection version of the Audi race engine, Team Bentley's sole car was fourth.

For the all-important third and final commitment in 2003, Bentley entered a couple of all-new Speed 8s, which were equipped with Michelin tyres rather than Dunlops. The decision to drop the earlier EXP (for experimental) part of the title indicated that the team recognised its two-year apprenticeship was over. It was now or never. Expectations of success were helped by the absence of the official Audi team after a hat-trick of wins in 2000, 2001 and 2002, though the marque was still represented by private entries. But Bentley could not have wished for a better outcome when the No. 7 car of Guy Smith, Dindo Capello and Tom Kristensen led Johnny Herbert, Mark Blundell and David Brabham in car No. 8 to a one-two result. It was Bentley's first Le Mans win in 73 years.

Team Bentley celebrated in a style fully in keeping with the spirit of the Bentley Boys in the 1920s. The 2003 winner, accompanied by a couple of Blower Bentleys, was driven along the Champs Elysée in central Paris the following day. The Bentley Boys and their Speed 8, with slick racing tyres, and no road licence, were cheered by thousands of Parisians. Two days later, the celebratory dinner at the Savoy Hotel in London was a faithful echo of the event thrown for Bentley after its 1927 Le Mans win. They were entirely fitting emotional responses to Team Bentley's great achievement. Franz-Josef Paefgen, who took over as Bentley chairman and chief executive after Tony Gott defected to BMW's Project Rolls-Royce, declared: 'This is one of the greatest moments in our company's long history.'

Indeed, the achievement would have been unimaginable when Bentley was owned by Rolls-Royce or Vickers. What remained unsaid was that the victory was only possible because of the Volkswagen takeover of Bentley and the racing technology that then flowed into the team from Audi. The headlines reflected another British victory – just as they did in W.O.'s days – but the reality was a reflection of the truly international nature of the car industry and modern motor racing.

By the time Bentley drivers were back on the winners' podium at Le Mans once more, the company had had another prominent and satisfied owner for a year. Britain's Queen Elizabeth II was formally presented with her Bentley state limousine by Paefgen at Windsor Castle in June 2002 to celebrate her Golden Jubilee as monarch. The car, a gift from a Bentley-led consortium of the country's specialist engineering companies, is not a stretched version of the Arnage. It is a unique model that is going to have to stay in service for 25 years or more. In other words, its designers had to avoid any transient design themes that could easily date.

The state limousine is the work of Crispin Marshfield, a senior Bentley designer whose proposal was selected by the queen at the end of 2000. That meant there was a tight schedule in order to design, engineer and construct the car in time for the jubilee festivities. The design called for a clever amalgam of tradition and modernity. Like the earlier series of Phantom state limousines made by Rolls-Royce, the latest car had to have raised rear seating and a very large glass area to enable the occupants to see and be seen. Naturally, though, the new car had to look like a Bentley, which required it to be a little longer and lower than previous state limousines. The lower roofline was achieved without compromising the headroom thanks to the use of unitary body construction rather than the body-on-frame construction of the earlier Phantoms.

Bentley used the car to provide the first indications of its future design direction. The car has flowing lines, well-rounded corners and definite haunches. It is about as sporty-looking as a state limousine can get. The front features large inner headlights and smaller outer lights, a treatment

Major attraction. Bentley had nearly 3,500 orders for the Continental GT when it went on sale in middle-2003. They represented a year's work at the Crewe factory.

reminiscent of some of the post-war cars. The radiator grille is unmistakably Bentley. However, in contrast to the company's recent trend and in a reflection of earlier policy, the grille is finished in bright metal, not body-coloured.

Designer Marshfield reflected: 'I was lucky to be given almost total freedom to design the car the way I wanted, something that would never happen with a production car that typically needs to be mass produced. In many ways from a designer's point of view, it was the dream job.'

So, Bentley was really buzzing under Volkswagen direction. Crewe had a new management team and new working practices. The company re-engineered the Arnage, successfully went motor racing at the highest level, and created a car fit for a queen. Above all, though, the company was focused on the development of the range that would become the cornerstone of its strategy after 2003. The plan was to create a new generation of cars, starting with a two-door coupé and following that with a four-door saloon and a two-door convertible at some time in the future.

The new range was initially known as MSB, or medium-sized Bentley, but the title was dropped when it became clear the cars would be virtually the size of the more expensive Arnage. At prices anticipated to be around $170,000/£100,000, the new cars would clearly have greater buyer accessibility than the Arnage, an altogether more exclusive range that cost half as much again. Over time, the lower prices of the newcomer were forecast to drive Bentley annual sales up to around 9,000, or nearly three

How times change: The interior of a Vintage Bentley (above) is in sharp contrast to expectations in the early 21st century. The rear seats opposite are normally occupied by Queen Elizabeth II and the Duke of Edinburgh.

times more than Crewe had ever produced in a single year. That would be a challenge. Neither was the new range destined to signal the early demise of the Arnage, which was increasingly bought with expensive (and profitable) customisation conversions by Bentley's Mulliner coachbuilding subsidiary. There would be cohabitation for a considerable time even after the arrival of the Continental four-door in 2005.

Volkswagen did more or less what Rolls-Royce did after buying Bentley in 1931. It started from scratch and appropriated components from its existing technology resources. Bentley purists may have shuddered, but component-sharing reflected the realities of the car industry by the end of the last century. When Rolls-Royce revealed its 2003 Phantom, for example, it had a V12 engine provided by its new parent company, BMW.

In the case of the 2003 Continental GT, it relies on a version of the same body-chassis unit that is used for the Volkswagen Phaeton saloon. Similarly, the Bentley uses versions of the Phaeton's four-wheel-drive system, six-speed automatic gearbox and 6-litre W12 engine. However, the Bentley is equipped with twin turbochargers and has 550 horsepower, nearly a third more than the Phaeton. While Bentley cars and their engines are assembled in Crewe, the body-chassis and most other key components are sourced from Volkswagen companies or its suppliers in Germany.

There were cavils from some commentators that the Continental is a sham, a commoner masquerading as a king. Indeed, logic says the Phaeton, at two-thirds of the price of a Continental GT, is the more sensible buyer choice. But that ignores the emotional appeal that certain brands have with the

public. The car may contain lots of Volkswagen bits, but the Continental GT is a Bentley, with all that implies in social cachet. The Phaeton is a beautifully engineered limousine that is unlikely to reach the company's sales forecasts because it is a Volkswagen in Mercedes-Benz and BMW territory. The Continental GT is a beautifully engineered coupé that seems destined to sell very well because it carries extremely classy badges.

With its thoroughly modern engineering bricks as a base, then, Bentley was able to craft a 21st-century high performance car in the spirit of its 20th-century ancestors. The brief was to create the fastest four-seater in the world, just as the 1950s Continental was. The design of the Continental GT is usually attributed to Dirk van Braeckel, the Belgian who became Bentley director of design in April 1999. In fact, the exterior design selected was by a young Brazilian who was recruited by van Braeckel and the interior became the responsibility of a young Englishman who was already working for Rolls-Royce and Bentley at the time of the 1998 split.

Raul Pires was a designer for Volkswagen in São Paulo before he was assigned to the group's European operations. Like van Braeckel, he worked in the Skoda studios immediately before the transfer to Bentley in the middle of 1999. It was a steep learning curve for Pires, who had never even seen a Bentley in his home country. As he immersed himself in the culture of the British marque though books and the Internet, his first encounter with the legendary Continental R was shortly after he began working at Crewe. It proved a turning point. Bentley's racing exploits in the 1920s also particularly appealed to Pires, a motor-racing enthusiast who, as a teenager, used to cycle

"Queen Elizabeth's state limousine is a unique model that is going to have to stay in service for 25 years or more. In other words, its designers had to avoid any transient design themes that could easily date"

the eight kilometres to the Interlagos circuit near São Paulo. 'It didn't take much to fall in love with the Bentley brand,' Pires later confessed.

Crewe's four-strong design department at the time of the takeover rose to 40 people over the following two years. They got more appropriate premises and facilities on another part of the site. Robin Page, an engineering and fine arts graduate of Coventry University and a former Jaguar apprentice, joined Bentley in 1995. He did much of the design work for the special cars commissioned from Mulliner by Prince Jefri of Brunei. Page's proposals won the internal competition to design the interior of the new Continental. It evolved from a simple, symmetrical sketch that aped the winged-B Bentley logo. 'If you can capture your design in two or three lines, you've got it,' said Page, explaining his success.

The 1950s Continental inspired the GT's big headlights, giant wheels, pronounced swage lines, rear wheel arches and long, low bodywork. However, the earlier car's sloping rear end treatment could not be repeated for reasons of high-speed stability. In fact, with the new car capable of over 190 mph, a discrete, pop-up spoiler behind the rear window and rear diffuser had to be incorporated into the design. The 1920s look of the mesh grille is instantly recognisable, even though the surround is body-coloured and slopes backwards more than any Bentley grille ever has. Volkswagen's product strategy committee under Piëch also decided against an alternative interior proposal that would have been more faithful to Bentleys of old. They rejected a modern interpretation of the old Continental R fascia – a simple piece of wood with instruments and controls inserted in a practical fashion – in favour of one that captures the luxury aura that today's customers expect.

The car that van Braeckel, Pires and Page created was universally praised. But with more than eight decades separating the Continental GT from W.O. Bentley's original 3-litre, how faithful is the lineage?

From the start, Bentleys were fast, but not furious. Their performance was effortless, their reliability total. Though they were big, strong cars, they remained dignified, elegant and confident. In clothing terms, they were the automotive equivalent of the understated London tailoring of Savile Row, in contrast to the Hugo Boss precision that might be represented by Porsche or the Versace flashiness of Lamborghini.

The first Bentleys were products of their time, which meant speed and reliability. If W.O.'s cars were not fast enough, he designed bigger engines for them. It was as simple as that. Like all the early motoring pioneers, the founder of Bentley gave scant attention to fuel consumption, exhaust emissions, noise levels and crash-worthiness when he created his cars.

Final inspection: A Continental GT receives minute scrutiny prior to customer delivery. The intense lighting helps to pinpoint any blemishes.

While its essence was distilled by its founder, 'Bentley' is not a static commodity. Parents pass their DNA to their children, but those children are not replicas of their parents. Thus, few of the products sold as Bentleys remained faithful to W.O.'s ideals once he severed connections with the company. Pushrod-operated valves replaced his overhead camshaft-driven multi-valve arrangements, V-type engines took over from the in-line units favoured by W.O., and turbocharging ousted the natural aspiration that the founder considered crucial. Some changes, though, were part of the natural evolution of the car during a period of great innovation. Unitary body construction, disc brakes and electronic controls were unknown to W.O.

Though his products were seldom at the forefront of new technology, which transformed the way cars were designed and manufactured last century, it is impossible to imagine he would not have embraced the necessary change if things had turned out differently for him. As it was, W.O. owned Bentley for less than seven years before Barnato bought it. When Rolls-Royce took over, W.O. was completely sidelined. In fact, he had very little influence at Bentley for most of its existence, but his name is still spoken of with reverence.

Showing the flag: When Smith/Kristensen/Capello triumphed at Le Mans in 2003, it was Bentley's first victory since 1930. The win helped to rebuild the Bentley name.

In spite of the inadequacies perpetrated by the various companies and individuals who controlled the Bentley name over the years, they must collectively have done things right for it to survive at all. It is almost a miracle that it did. Hundreds of car marques that were in existence when W.O. started his company are forgotten footnotes in today's history books. By the end of the last century, the real power in the international motor industry was held by a handful of giant groups that were themselves the results of great transcontinental mergers or the astonishing post-war industrialisation of Japan and South Korea. Of the current survivors whose names W.O. would

> ❝How many people can say, hand on heart, 'I don't like Bentleys'? One can almost guarantee that other car companies, no matter how exalted their reputations, will produce more divisive responses to similar questions❞

have recognised, only family firms like Fiat, Ford and Peugeot have any direct connections with those early motoring days.

Despite the tortuous evolution, though, the spirit of Bentley survived, personified by the Continental GT. The marque is still held in great affection among car enthusiasts, particularly in Britain. How many people can say, hand on heart, 'I don't like Bentleys'? One can almost guarantee that other car companies, no matter how exalted their reputations, will produce more divisive responses to similar questions. Does that affection stem from those early Vintage cars and their great racing achievements, from the series of beautiful Derby Bentleys, or from that rare Continental R Type momentarily glimpsed as a child? Whatever it was remains powerful today.

Bentley remains a worthy motoring option in an arena of Rolls-Royce and Maybach, BMW and Mercedes, Aston Martin and Maserati. It would not have been the case if the Volkswagen group had applied the same formula it once did to its many products. The Golf hatchback was the genesis of the Skoda Octavia and Seat Leon – models that looked similar, contained more equipment and cost less to buy. However, while the Continental GT is in a class of its own, it could create a problem for Bentley in the future, a problem understood only too well by the producers of Calvin Klein tee shirts and Burberry scarves. By making their products both aspirational and affordable, they attract many customers who do their brand images no favours. A marque like Bentley, which reeks of class and old money, may face a similar dilemma because of the Continental GT's unique combination of respectability, performance, rarity and affordability. If it is bought by a surfeit of undereducated footballers, talentless pop stars, TV nonentities and drug dealers, a reputation that was so hard to re-establish could become tarnished once more.

INDEX

1912 Peugeot, 39

1914 Mercedes Grand Prix car, 38

1948 Bentley Cresta, 104

Aston Martin, 54, 69, 115, 155

Autocar, 32, 38, 40, 55

Barnato, Woolf "Babe," 32, 33, 43, 47, 48, 51, 52,
    57, 58–60, 64, 69

Bentley, W. O., 16, 19, 21–22, 26–28, 30, 32, 33,
    38, 42, 44, 47, 52, 53, 58, 60, 65, 68, 72, 74, 77,
    78, 83, 91, 135, 144, 152–154

Bentley Boys, 23, 30, 32, 46, 55, 57, 145, 146

Bentley models:

    Arnage, 131, 146, 148

    Blower 46, 145

    Blue Train, 58, 59

    Continental GT, 8–10, 11, 14–16, 19, 20, 71, 111, 117, 138, 140,
    147–149, 152, 153

    Continental R, 11–13, 21, 83, 93, 104–108,
        110, 122–124, 126, 149, 155

    CXA, 122

    Derby, 70, 77–79, 155

    EXP1, 26, 37

    Green Label, 140

    Mk V, 85

    Mk VI, 75, 80, 81, 83, 85, 88, 89, 95, 99,
        103, 104

    Mulsanne series, 119, 125, 129

    Red Label, 140, 141

    S series, 86, 87, 90, 91, 111

    S3, 92, 110

    T series, 93, 99, 100

    Turbo R, 115–118, 122

Bentley Motors, 9, 21, 23, 27, 32, 33, 42–44, 47,
    50, 53, 55, 59–61, 64, 65, 68, 69, 138

Birkin, Henry "Tim," 10, 47, 50–53, 55, 59,
    74, 117

Blatchley, John, 94–97, 105, 106, 110

Blundell, Mark, 145

BMW, 10, 11

Brabham, David, 145

Braeckel, Dirk van, 16, 149, 152

Brooklands, 30

Burgess, Frank, 38

Campbell, Malcolm, 28

Capello, Dindo, 145, 154

Carruth, Jack, 64

Clement, Frank, 55

Corniche, 77, 82, 83, 93, 101, 117, 121, 122

Cricklewood, 71, 72, 78

Crosby, Gordon F., 38, 40–43

D. Napier & Sons, 54, 64, 65, 71

Daimler, 54, 144

Depression, 51, 60, 61, 79

Dickson, Doug, 10

Duff, John, 55

Duller, George, 22, 23

Eichhorn, Ulrich, 10

Freestone & Webb, 44, 46, 52, 53

Frére, Patrick, 64

Gott, Tony, 131, 141

Grand Prix, 50

Greenley, Ken, 118, 119, 122, 123

Gurney Nutting, 46, 94, 110

Gurney Nutting-bodied six-speed coupe, 62, 63

Hallmark, Adrian, 10

Harrow, Dale, 55

Heffernan, John, 118, 119, 122

Herbert, Johnny, 145

Humber, 54

Hutton, Ray, 16

Isle of Man, 30

Java, 132, 133

Kristensen, Tom, 145, 154

Lagonda, 34, 45, 54, 68, 69, 72, 115

Lamborghini, 11

Lanchester, 54

Le Mans, 16, 24, 25, 29, 30, 33, 40, 45–51, 55, 58,
    59, 69, 116, 133, 135, 137, 141–146, 154

Loraine, 29

Marinetti, Filippo Tommaso, 37

Marshfield, Crispin, 146, 147

Medcalf, James D., 15

Mercedes-Benz, 11, 30, 93, 130, 149

Montlhéry, 30

Morris, Graham, 133, 140

Napier-Bentley, 64

Olympia, 61

Paulin, George, 82, 83

Paulo, São, 149, 152, 155

Piëch, Ferdinand, 11, 134, 135

Pires, Paul, 111, 149

Plastow, David, 114

Pontieu, 47

Porsche GB, 10

Pourtout Carrossier, 80

Project 11B VIII, 96

Raalte, Noel van, 42

RB-211 engine, 113

Rhodes, Cecil, 57

Ricardo, Harry, 52, 53

Robins, Ralph, 132

Rolls-Royce, 16, 20, 21, 26, 28, 34, 37, 44, 45, 54,
      60, 64, 65, 71, 72, 74, 78, 83, 85, 93, 97, 103,
      111, 124, 126, 129, 130, 146, 153, 155

Rolls-Royce models:

            Phantom II, 51, 61, 74, 82

            Silver Cloud, 94–97, 103, 105, 106, 110

            Silver Seraph, 131, 133

            Silver Shadow, 94, 96, 103, 113, 115, 129

            Silver Wraith, 83

Royce, Henry, 64, 65, 72, 74, 77

Seat Leon, 155

Segrave, Henry, 28

Skoda Octavia, 16, 20, 155

Smith, Guy, 145, 154

Stutz, 29

Sunbeam, 54

Team Bentley, 145

Thomas, Parry, 28

Varley, Harry, 38

Vickers, 11, 20, 101, 117, 124, 129, 130, 133, 134

Villiers, Amherst, 50

Volkswagen, 10, 11, 14, 54, 138, 148, 149

Volkswagen models:

            Phaeton, 148, 149

            Touareg, 11

Ward, Peter, 119, 130

World War II, 71, 74, 82, 83, 90, 94, 103

ACKNOWLEDGMENTS

Many people generously gave their wisdom and insights during my research for this book, and my previous book that inspired it, *Kidnap of the Flying Lady* (Motorbooks International, 2003). Among them were:

John Blatchley, Dirk van Braeckel, Thos. L. Bryant, Richard Charlesworth, John Crawford, Richard Dallimore, Doug Dickson, Ulrich Eichhorn, Tony Gott, Ken Greenley, Adrian Hallmark, Dale Harrow, John Heffernan, Ray Hutton, Crispin Marshfield, Graham Morris, John Nutter, Franz-Josef Paefgen, Robin Page, Sarah Perris, David Plastow, Paul Pires, Bernd Pischetsrieder, Tom Purves, David Rolfe, Peter Ward and Chris Woodwark. A number of other sources preferred anonymity.

Illustrations for this book were sourced from Bentley Motors, the W.O. Bentley Memorial Foundation, LAT, John Blatchley and Heffernan Design Associates.